Date Due

FEB 16			
NOV 27 1990			
ILLO			

THE WAIT LETTERS

Niagara Jail and Courthouse
Reproduction Courtesy Metropolitan Toronto Library Board

THE WAIT LETTERS

BY BENJAMIN WAIT

Introduction by Mary Brown
&
Afterword by Michael Cross

Press Porcépic Limited

This edition is published by Press Porcépic Limited, 70 Main Street, Erin,
Ontario, in October of 1976, with the assistance of the Canada Council
and the Ontario Arts Council. Printed in Canada.

ISBN 0-88878-060-5

1 2 3 4 5 81 80 79 78 77

Distribution:

CANADA	U.S.A.	U.K. & EUROPE
Musson Book Company	Books Canada Inc.	Books Canada Ltd.
30 Lesmill Road	33 East Tupper Street	1 Bedford Road
Don Mills, Ontario	Buffalo, N.Y.	London N.2,
M3B 2T6	14203	England

Canadian Shared Cataloguing in Publication Data

Wait, Benjamin, 1813-1895.
    The Wait Letters

ISBN 0-88878-060-5

1. Wait, Benjamin, 1813-1895. 2. Canada — History — Rebellion, 1837-1838. I. Brown, Mary, 1925-   II. Title

FC451.W3A4 1976   971.03'8'0924   C76-017195-5
F1032.W3A4 1976

TO THE READER

This is a "found novel". It is also a political prisoner's diary, an unorthodox chapter in Canadian history and a very rare book. Written in 1840 and published three years later, the Wait letters are reprinted here for the first time.[1]

About one year ago, I examined a hand-bound typescript at an auction in London, Ontario. Centred on the black leather cover, in gold letters, was a title *Extracts—Benjamin Wait's Narrative Canadian Rebellion 1838-42* and below, "published in Buffalo, N.Y. A.W. Wilgus, 1843". Inside, there were fifteen letters typed, rather badly, in blue ink. This was obviously a transcription from an old book (published thirty years before typewriters were invented). I was intrigued. I bid. I bought. That night, I read the letters at one sitting, as I hope you will. Perhaps, I thought, this was fiction disguised as fact, a "A Novel Found at an Auction". After all, Poe had used that device in his story "A MS Found in a Bottle" in 1833 and in 1850 Hawthorne used a similar trick in "The Custom House" chapter of *The Scarlet Letter*. Even the idea of writing a novel in the form of letters was not exactly new in 1843. Samuel Richardson invented that way of telling a story a century earlier. When I first read the typescript of the Wait letters, I suspected that it was a novel in the epistolary tradition. I was wrong, wrong at least to the extent that this book is not fiction but autobiography.

Later, I discovered that historians have known about Benjamin Wait for a long time. He was born in Canada and lived in York, on the Grand River, in Upper Canada, a settlement about forty miles west of Niagara. In 1837, he was twenty-four, married and the father of an infant daughter. Although York was Tory country, his sympathies were with the Reformers led by William Lyon Mackenzie. Shortly after the abortive affair at Montgomery's Tavern on December 7th, 1837, and Mackenzie's escape, Benjamin Wait left his home to join the Reform forces in the western part of the province. Their headquarters was the tavern of Jacob Beemer in Scotland, near Burford. (Beemer comes off rather badly in Wait's letters as an informer in prison and so perhaps it is only fair to record his earlier contribution here.)

Wait probably stopped at Scotland on his way to London where he arrived about December 13th to find the reformers scattered. He then fled to Navy Island in the Niagara River and spent Christmas there; when that island was evacuated, he proceeded to Coneaut, Ohio and subsequently to Schlosser. He was captured during the Short Hills raid on June 21st, 1838, and jailed in Niagara. The leader of that raid, Colonel Morrow (or Moreau) was hanged on July 30th. On August 11th, Wait was sentenced to hang "for high treason" along with Chandler and McLeod. Jacob Beemer shortly received the same sentence. The date set for Wait's execution was August 25th. He lived to tell his story only because his wife, Maria, travelled seven hundred miles to Quebec and back between August 11th and 23rd to plead for his life with the Governor General, the Earl of Durham. His stay of execution arrived just thirty minutes before the deadline set by the court. Two more reprieves were granted before he was moved from the Niagara jail to prisons in Kingston (Fort Henry), Quebec, Liverpool, Portsmouth and Van Dieman's Land, a British convict colony south of Australia, now called Tasmania after Tasman, a seventeenth century Dutch navigator who explored the island. Benjamin Wait escaped in December or January of 1842 aboard an American whaling ship and seven months later was reunited with his family at Niagara Falls, N.Y. In 1843 he published *Letters from Van Dieman's Land, written during four years' imprisonment for political offences comitted in Upper Canada....*[2]

Those are the facts. There is, however, another story about *The Wait Letters* which makes this Canadian diary even more curious. The typescript from which this book is printed originally belonged to the Leonard estate. The Leonards were an old London family who came to Canada from Massachusetts in 1829 and set up a foundry in the village of London in 1838. Elijah Leonard, the son of the original settler, became a member of the Legislative Council in 1862 (on the Reform ticket) and a Senator of the Dominion in 1867. He married Emeline Woodman, also of London, the daughter of another "rebel" who, like Wait, was transported to Van Dieman's Land. Woodman was pardonned in 1845 but died on the ship which was bringing him home. His letters, pardon and other documents were treasured by Emeline Woodman Leonard and one of her sons, Frank E. Leonard, added to them other material relevent to the 1837-38 rebellion, especially as it related to London.[3] Leonard had typed copies made of his grandfather's letters etc. and of extracts from books by other exiles. One of these books was the one by Benjamin Wait.[4]

Exciting as history, the letters are equally fascinating as literature. Letters, like soliloquies, have their own authorities; the reader tends to believe that what they say is true, at least from the writer's point of view and to identify with the first person narrator. By including other documents, such as the note from Hume, the appeal to Lord Russell and a copy of his Ticket of Leave, Wait added to his credibility. His reports of conditions in prisons and on the convict ships are historically verifiable, as are his descriptions of the hundreds of English children jailed and even exiled for minor crimes. Wait's observations of the system which condoned these social evils may shock but not surprise anyone familiar with the novels of Charles Dickens.

Even though the date of the first letter makes it clear that Wait was not executed but exiled, the reader is held by the skilful arrangement of the details of his escape from the gallows; it is almost as though Wait was only a witness to the events he describes. Time past is juxtaposed with time present. The chronology is rearranged to anticipate a crisis, to interpret a motive, develop a character or setting. This use of double time allows for an interplay of narration and recollection, of statement and analysis and produces a tension we associate with fiction. Partly because the anguish of his months in prison was recorded in the relative tranquility of exile, Wait was able to give his narrative dramatic shape.

From the first sentence of the first letter:

You, Benjamin Wait, shall be taken from the court to the place from whence you last came, and there remain until the 25th of August, when, between the hours of 11 and 1, you shall be drawn on a hurdle to the place of execution, and there hanged by the neck, until you are dead, and your body shall be quartered.

to the end of the last letter, the suspense never falters. In the final letter, the villain of earlier events in Canada, Sir George Arthur, is revealed to be the same "Bloody Executioner" who signed fifteen hundred death warrants in Van Dieman's Land during his tenure as Governor there from 1824-36.[5] If this were fiction, one might say the writer had leaned rather heavily on coincidence!

Few of the "characters" are stereotyped. Sir George Arthur is more than a simple villain. He is a fanatic and a martinet. The Earl of Durham is not a hero but a reluctant *deus ex machina* with a headache. Jacob Beemer, although he is a fellow exile, is a vulgar man, a deceiver and an informer. Maria is the heroine responsible for saving her husband's life, but because Wait lets her tell the story herself, in her own letter, she becomes a complex character, a dedicated, aggressive, rather humourless lady. I could not help thinking, as I read her letter, that she and Susanna Moodie would have scratched each other's eyes out if they had met in 1838. For the Moodies, the rebellion meant army pay and J. W. Dunbar Moodie was better at fighting than farming. While he was away in the militia, Susanna wrote patriotic verse. One example will give the flavour of those poems though it will do nothing to enhance her literary reputation. Imagine Maria Wait's reaction to

    The Convict's Wife
Pale Matron! I see thee in agony steep
The pillow on which thy young innocents sleep;

Who murmur in slumber the dear cherished name
Of that sire who has covered his offspring with shame;

Of that husband whom justice has wrenched from thy side,
Of the wretch who the laws of this country defied—

No hope speeds thy thoughts as they traverse the wave,
To the far distant land of Exile and Slave![6]

Maria Wait and Susanna Moodie conveniently illustrate the political polarization of the period. Benjamin Wait is a "rebel" or a "patriot" depending on your point of view. There is no doubt, however, that he is the hero of this remarkable book. He engages our sympathy because he is prepared to fight and ready to die for his beliefs with courage and without self pity. There is even a certain charming bravura in his confrontations with a number of "petty officers" and a nice sense of irony in his account of the appalling conditions in various prisons.

But while we identify with him, both as story teller and hero, he directs our attention elsewhere. For him, the focus is not a man but a country tragically endangered by political patronage and corruption. He was, of course, not alone. Elijah Woodman, in a letter to his father from Van Dieman's Land, dated July 4, 1843, wrote, "...a man had better be a slave than for the whole population to be in bondage to the power that then was."[7] The theme, then, not the persona, is Wait's focal point and it becomes so for the reader as well. "Reform never dies" is a motto Wait borrows from Bacon for the title page of his book and his unremitting conviction of the justice of his cause enabled him to endure his imprisonment and exile.

It may come as a shock to realize that nearly all the "characters" in the book were alive when it was first published in 1843. Lord Durham was the exception; after his resignation in 1838, he returned to England and died there in 1840. Sir John Franklin was dismissed from his post as Governor in Van Dieman's Land in 1843 and two years later set out on his last Arctic voyage. He died on June 11th, 1847, in Canada's frozen north. Sir George Arthur lived until 1854. Benjamin Wait survived all his enemies and many of his friends. He died at eighty-two years of age in 1895.

M.M. Brown
University of Western Ontario,

I wish to express my thanks to the University of Western Ontario, the Canada Council, Dr. Clara Thomas, Edward Phelps and Beth Miller of the D.B. Weldon Library at Western and to Archibald Campbell of the National Library.

---

[1] Wait's was the *first* of nine accounts to be published by exiles, not all of whom were Canadians. Mr. Archibald Campbell of the National Library has discovered that only twenty-two copies of Wait's book are known to exist in Canadian Libraries.

² Published in Buffalo by A.W. Wilgus in 1843. In the Introduction, Wait explains that the letters were composed at monthly intervals, beginning three months after his arrival in Van Diemen's Land. They were written "to Thaddeus Smith, Esq. of Canada West" and when the book was published, it was dedicated to Smith "as a slight token of regard due to him; for the more than fraternal generosity extended to his (Wait's) family during the captivity of the author."

³ The Woodman story was reconstructed by historian Fred Landon in *An Exile from Canada*, first published in 1960 by Longman's, Green and Co.

⁴ With some editorial revisions and some additions from the original book, F.E. Leonard's typescript is reproduced here as *The Wait Letters*. The order of the letters remains the same. This book differs from the original in the omission of a long, polemical introduction on the necessity for reform, two letters by Wait and several letters by Maria Wait which describe her unsuccessful attempts in England to have her husband pardonned.

⁵ Dr. Landon quotes official records during Arthur's regime which give a figure of 260 death warrants. The truth probably lies somewhere between the two figures. There is no doubt, however, that Arthur's departure from Van Diemen's Land was the cause for celebration by both prisoners and settlers. He was heartily disliked. His next posting was Upper Canada.

⁶ Published in *The Literary Garland*, (Montreal), Vol. III, April, 1841. It is interesting to note that Mrs. Moodie's sister, Agnes Strickland, seems to have been kindly disposed to Wait and the other Canadians when they were on board the prison ship in Portsmouth in January, 1839. The reference is in the letter dated March, 1841.

⁷ F. Landon, *An Exile from Canada*, p.220.

Reform never dies
　　　　—Bacon

1

Battle of Short Hills and Capture

At the first intimation of the rising near Toronto, I armed and left my home, at York, on the Grand River, without a regret; all ardency to mingle in the strife for freedom; and proceeded towards a known point of concentration. Indeed, it was highly necessary for me to be on the move, or, at least, on the "qui vive;" for my well known radical principles, rendered me unsafe at home; while the circumstance of the absence of my wife and child, on a visit at my father's, sixty miles distant, was, to my high tory neighbors, proof sufficient of a premeditated arrangement. My limits will not permit me to go into a detail; and I will, therefore, merely add, that I arrived in the London District just in time to witness the unhappy dispersion, when it became necessary for every one to shift for himself. I therefore retraced my steps, which had to be done with the utmost care and vigilance I travelled mostly by night, and finally arrived on the frontiers, despite the thousand dangers that beset me, after having been twice intercepted—once by Indians, whose chief, a particular friend, let me go, having been attracted by a red rose, the badge of loyalty, which I had providentially picked up and pinned on my cap: and once by a band of drunken volunteer guards, from whom, by a daring manouver, I made a happy escape. On Christmas eve, *gallantly assisted by patriotic ladies* I launched an old canoe upon the Niagara, and crossed to the Land of Freedom, from whence I soon found my way to Navy Island, where I partook a cheerful Christmas dinner beneath the banner of the sister stars. At the evacuation of the place, I proceded with the melee as far as Coneaut, Ohio, where, by the virulence of three seated inward inflammations, caused by continued exposure, I lay for several weeks, but one remove from the grave, under the charge of the noble and generous minded Dr. Raymond, to whom, with the families of H. Lake Esq., and the Rev. J.J. Bliss, I would here offer the sincere tribute of a grateful heart.

From Coneaut I returned, by stage, to Schlosser, where I happily found my wife and child, who received me almost as one from the dead. In the mean time Sir George Arthur displaced Sir Francis, in Upper Canada; and soon after, the Earl of Durham arrived, as Governor General of the Canadas; from whose administration proceedings, scarcely consistent with our future plans, were anticipated. Consequently, twenty-six, all *Canadians*, daring fellows, ready to be sacrificed in the field or on the scaffold, penetrated, doubly armed, without hope of return to the heart of the enemy's country, surrounded on every side by the regular infantry, lancers, volunteers, and Indians, (where a few Americans came to us,) on a secret mission—the object of which I am not yet at liberty to detail—to which, however, let it suffice that I declare there was nothing in the slightest degree dishonorable or disreputable attached, notwithstanding subsequent surmise and evil report.

After a trifling, successful irruption upon a company of insulting orange lancers, &c. far outnumbering us, whom we took, detained a short time, then dismissed, our little band retreated and dispersed, when a part were captured and sent, with twenty or more of the innocent inhabitants, to a jail, where we were all separately indicted for High Treason, by having appeared "armed with swords, spears, muskets, bayonets, rifles, pistols, and other offensive weapons, against the peace of her Majesty, Victoria, by the grace of God, Queen of Great Britain and Ireland, with intent to do her some grievous harm." On this indictment the gallant Col. Morrow, for whose apprehension a reward of 250 pounds was paid, was hastily tried, found guilty, and murdered on the scaffold, with but a few days granted in which to arrange his worldly affairs. He died like a man, honored and mourned, a glorious martyr in the cause of truth and the rights of man. Here I ought to consider this long introduction as closed, and the request of my friends briefly complied with. Yet I must add, that the captured innocent citizens were acquitted; and sixteen of the participators sentenced to death upon the gallows. Thirteen of them however, received an immediate commutation, while three Messrs. Chandler, McLeod, and myself, with Beemer, who was soon after added, were reserved for positive execution.

Niagara Jail and Courthouse
Reproduction Courtesy Metropolitan Toronto Library Board

2

TRIAL AND REPRIEVE

Ashgrove, near Oatlands, V.D.L.
April, 1840.
"You, Benjamin Wait, shall be taken from the court to the place from whence you last came, and there remain until the 25th. of August, when, between the hours of 11 and 1, you shall be drawn on a hurdle to the place of execution, and there hanged by the neck, until you are dead, and your body shall be quartered. The Lord have mercy on your soul!!!"

Such was the horrid sentence passed upon me by Judge Jones, on the 11th August, 1838. It will be supposed that a doom of such ignominious import, must have made a deep impression upon my mind. But I firmly believe it created a greater, or at least, a more sensible effect upon the crowd of spectators, (for the house was literally crammed,) than within my breast; for I was prepared for the event, and fully persuaded that it would take place, despite the jury's recommendation to mercy, which was special, or the motion of my very able and active counsel, (Mr. Alexander Stewart,) to arrest the verdict, on the ground of an illegal jury; the foreman, (Mr. Wragg) being an alien, irrevocably so, by special act of Parliament. In fact, I should have been much disappointed, (though I must say, happily so,) if an arrest of verdict had been ruled; for on the day of my arrival in the jail of Niagara, I was informed by a gentleman high in government esteem, that I was "a man marked by an exasperated governor, as a fit subject to wreak his utmost vengeance upon;" and had I felt even a *hope* of favor, or that my case would not be regarded a desperate one, it would have been effectually dispelled by Sir George himself, who, (at the close of an interview in which he offered a free pardon and emolument, if I would give information of the combination, he knew existed in the country, for the subversion of the government, by which he hoped to obtain more subjects for "retributive justice,") said, "for your obstinacy, in refusing to make reparation to the country for the injury you have done it, you shall feel the rigor of that power you affect to despise, and be *hung* despite every effort to the contrary. Yes," said he, with the tremor of passion on his lip, "though the Province rise en masse, and beg it, you shall receive no favor from me." By such passionate threats, he had hoped to make my spirit quail beneath his *mighty* power, and force the desired information from me. But they were vain; and all I had to return was, that "all the *reparation* in my power I would make *instanter;* that was, as he considered me a prime instigator, my blood was at his service, if he would deem my execution atonement sufficient for all the others who had been incarcerated for conduct," he "considered me the mover of." Thus, then, these boding menaces, together with the sealed fate of the late Col. Morrow, insured to me the verdict and foregoing sentence and caused an apathy relative to it, and an indifference that, at this distant moment, makes me shudder.

But happily for the preservation of my life, and the lives of others, the sanguinary purposes of the Governor were frustrated, much to his chagrin, by the energetic conduct of my affectionate wife, who could not see the husband of her choice sacrificed to a despot's fury, without a struggle to save him. You will remember how fearlessly she overcame the obstacles thrown in her way; and counter to the advice, nay, persuasions of numerous self *styled* friends, proceeded to Quebec to procure, if possible, an interview with the Earl of Durham, of whom she had no doubt she could obtain a pardon, or at least, a commutation, by the strength of her entreaties—in which effort of generous affection she was deservedly successful. A detail of the obstructions thrown in her way, the difficulties she encountered, her feelings and the occurrances on the passage to and from Quebec, with her pleadings there, and interview with Sir George on her return, I will give you from her own pen, it being the copy of a letter she wrote a friend subsequent to my being sent from Niagara—a duplicate of which she gave me, when on a visit to me at Kingston—and which, with other of her letters, I have preserved with care, through every vicissitude.

Perhaps the indifference with which I listened to the ominous sentence, induced the authorities to treat me with greater severity than the others; for immediately after "guilty" was said by the foreman of the jury, I was hurried away to the iron bound stone cell, known in the jail as the "condemned cell;" and there locked up, consigned to the solitary musings of my own mind; and debarred from correspondence with my fellow prisoners, except what could pass through a small diamond in the iron door, and almost from the light of heaven. Here, in the hour of loneliness, the idea of my approaching death came over me. My life I never valued; and to sacrifice it in the cause of liberty, truth, and justice, was the end I most desired. I had calmly, in other times, counted the probabilities of such an event, and deemed the offering a voluntary and perchance a necessary one, upon the altar of legitimate rights. But I had never before considered it in connection with the desolation my fate would entail upon my family—or the sad and sorrowful adieus that must be given—the tears and grief of a wife—the bereavement of a dear child—and a separation from the friends of my happy days. The thoughts were bitter, and created an agony of mind that only gave way to the pure and holy influences of religion, which can alone produce that proper resignation to the Divine will in the last trial of nature, and afford the peace and consolation so requisite to sustain the soul and raise it above the vicissitudes of mortality.

Though Mrs. Wait had left Niagara with a strong hope of success in her mission to Lord Durham, yet I did not for a moment cherish the thought—knowing that his Lordship had, while on a recent visit to Upper Canada, refused to comply with the petitions of many of the inhabitants, and extend to that Province the general amnesty he had proclaimed in Lower Canada; or interfere at that time, with the administration of the Lieut. Governor—consequently made every preparation in my power for the approaching hour of dissolution; and even when Mrs. Wait returned with the assurance, both from the Governor General and Sir George, that a respite was granted, I felt still incredulous, and up to the latest moment gave no heed to the flatteries of hope; and subsequent discoveries described in Mrs. Wait's letters, will show you that my incredulity was not without foundation, although the sequel did result propitiously.

Previous to my sentence, and subsequent to Mrs. Wait's return from Quebec, she resided near the jail to administer as much as possible to our relief; therefore I suffered nothing from the want of provisions or clothing, but unabated mental distress through the daily prospect of the inhumanity of the jailer, who had driven her from the gratings several times in the day, lest she might communicate some intelligence unheard by him. By the orders of the Sheriff she has also been detained, at the gate of the yard, and refused admittance by the armed guard, who, with the heart of a dastard, presented a bayonet at her breast and drove her back. These orders were given, as was afterwards stated by sheriff Hamilton, in answer to a request for an explanation, by the Judge on the bench, when she made an appeal to him through my attorney, who said it was "on account of having received information from a James Gordon, that her admittance to the prison would endanger the safety of the prisoners," &c. &c. Such an explanation offered a fine opportunity for Mr. Stewart to exert his talent at satire, which was improved, to the no small amusement of every generous mind present, and annoyance of the Sheriff. An order emanated from the bench at once for her admission to the grates of the prison; still she was subject to the malevolence of the wretch who kept the jail. After the respite was ordered, I made this conduct the subject of a petition to the Lieut. Governor, who ventured no reply until after I was removed to Kingston, when the board of magistrates was called together, and the letter laid before them, without the knowledge of myself or any one friendly person. The consequence was, that, on the testimony of old Wheeler, his son, and the turnkeys, the petition was pronounced a "libel." The result of this meeting of the board, was first communicated to Mrs. Wait by Mr. Macaulay, Private Secretary to Arthur, when she called at Toronto on her way to Kingston, who appeared highly incensed that such a "false statement should be made against any officer in discharge of his duty." He exhibited the petition to her, as she had heard or seen nothing of it before, when she declared every statement was true; and would appeal to a number of gentlemen of veracity; but nothing farther would be done about it, yet I must bear the odium of a "libel." The 24th regiment was our guard, and was commanded by brevet Major Townsend, rendered famous in the annals of Irish crim. con. by the eloquence of the noted Irish Barrister,—Phillips. He often visited our cells with no other apparent design than to insult us. His arbitrary and cowardly spirit was contemptibly manifested, by refusing Mrs. Wait permission to cross the Niagara River, when I was undergoing an examination at the Ontario House, Niagara Falls. His regiment was afterwards exchanged for the 43d, the character of whose commander, Col. Boothe, formed an exalted contrast to that of his predecessor in charge. The secret is, Boothe was a christian and a soldier, while the other was dissolute and cowardly.

I scarce need remind you that there were sixteen "brave faithful, and honest men," limited to a life of two weeks at the same special assize at which I was sentenced—poor Morrow having been executed previous to our arraignment—and soon after three others were added to our number. Of these, thirteen received a commutation of sentence, and were sent away to Fort Henry, at Kingston, on 21st August, leaving four, Messrs. Chandler, McLeod, Beemer and myself, for positive execution, and one for mercy. When they were separated from us and manacled for their journey, the scene became replete with sorrow—tears rolled from the eyes of the poor fellows who supposed they were bidding us adieu for ever— the cheeks of manhood were blanched with grief, and there was more dejection in the hearts of those whose lives were to be prolonged in slavery, than amongst us for whom there was no hope. They parted from us as from dying companions, with whom they had long suffered. One agonizing sensation pervaded every soul, the intensity of which none can have an adequate conception, but those who have felt its saddening influence. The scenes of my incarceration, trial and sentence, were all enacted within what I might call my native District—consequently intense interest was excited. Petitions for a pardon or commutation were prepared, universally signed, and placed in the hands of my father, who, though feeble from ill health, proceeded, accompanied by the Rev. Mr. Johnson, of Drummondville, to Toronto, to lay them before the Governor, whom, they on arrival, were informed, had left the seat of government some days previous, on an excursion through the remote parts of his government—perhaps a visit to Lower Canada—and would not return until after the expiration of the time determined upon for our execution. From Toronto, my father's ill health obliged him to return; but the benevolent Mr. Johnson continued on to Kingston, vainly hoping to meet or hear from Arthur there. He too returned, well convinced that the Governor had designedly left Toronto, at that critical moment, to evade a recurrence of the like appeals in this case, which had given him so much annoyance, and the people so much reason for censure, in the cases of the lamented Lount and Matthews; and the subsequent conduct of his Excellency seems to place such convictions beyond a doubt.

Preparations were making for the final performances, and a Jack Ketch forwarded from Toronto, to do a deed for us he had done for Lount and Matthews. This was a precaution taken by the Sheriff to prevent the necessity of acting himself as executioner, which he did in Morrow's case, after a hundred dollar bribe had failed to induce a black man to act for him. This Jack was kept about the jail, not daring to leave it until it was found there would be no "work in his way," when he was driven from the yard and never after heard of.

The 22nd brought Mrs. Wait from Quebec with intelligence of a respite, but no intimation of it had been made at the proper office. She went to Toronto on the following day, but no satisfaction was to be given her there as you will see by her letter. The final day arrived—the hour came that limited the time—and at last half past twelve brought the Sheriff from Kingston, where, after he had delivered the prisoners at Fort Henry, he met the Governor, whom he waited on and inquired "what must be done for the poor men in Niagara, for whom he hoped a respite might be extended?" Sir George detained him until the last boat upward bound for the day, had put off, then gave him an order. Should he wait until the following day, the hour for our execution would be passed at his peril; and the execution of Morrow had made such an impression upon his mind, that he was glad of the respite, and determined to make an effort to obtain the Governor's boat; in which he was successful after considerable altercation, and succeeded in gaining the Niagara dock at half past twelve, P.M. where the Rev. Mr. Creen met and received the happy tidings, which he communicated to us as soon as possible. It would appear by this elusive conduct of the Governor, that he had determined to execute us at all hazards, and then lay the blame at the door of some of his officials, for he wished it believed that he had left an order for a respite in Toronto; and no doubt, had this ruse succeeded, a despatch charging the blame to some petty official, would have been a full exculpation for him in Downing street; but his temerity was scarce adequate to this step. The respite extended to six days only, yet it created a complete reversion in my breast; for I had never known but few cases of an execution taking place after a respite had once been granted. So I thought no more of being "hung" but set myself at work vigorously to oppose transportation, which I knew to be illegal.

But I must here close, to give room for Mrs. Wait's communication.

I remain, dear sir,
Yours, &c. &c.

3

MRS. WAIT'S APPEAL TO LORD DURHAM

Niagara, U.C.
October 15, 1838.

My Dear Friend,

During the trial of my husband, I had vainly hoped the jury would, as they were inclined, find some technical point on which to hang a plea for acquittal, but with no other reason than the fond desire of an excited and anxious mind. The fatal verdict aroused me from this delusion, and I at once determined to proceed to Quebec, procure, if possible, an interview with the Earl of Durham, and plead with all the energy of an afflicted heart, for the life of him with whose destiny mine was so nearly linked.

Therefore, I set about, with the utmost alacrity, preparing for the arduous duty. On the evening after the sentence of death was pronounced, I communicated to my husband's attorney, my intention of appealing to Lord Durham; but he thought that his Lordship would not interfere with the administration of Sir George Arthur, who would doubtless feel the more exasperated by an appeal to his superior in authority. This too, was the opinion of all those to whom I had looked for counsel; and even their entreaties were used to prevent my leaving Niagara. They argued, that as the time allotted for my husband to live was short, I had better remain and afford him all the consolation in my power, I had an infant, also, whose life might be endangered, either by speedy travelling, at that season of the year, or by being deprived of her natural nourishment, in case I left her; that petitions would assuredly be forwarded to Sir George, and every thing possible done for the unhappy prisoners.

These were the persuasions adduced, but far was it from me to delay, and vainly seek the life of my husband at the blood-stained hands of Arthur, from whom I could not expect even a particle of mercy. My babe was kissed, left with a friend, and committed to the protecting care of Him who ever watches over the orphan and the widow, for even this, we had too much reason to fear, would be our lot, and which, if possible I was determined to make a desperate effort to prevent. It was considered perfectly useless to entertain the slightest hope for the life, either of Mr. Wait or Mr. Chandler, the former being marked by the Governor, as I was repeatedly told, for the extremity of the law, while the latter, on account of his advanced age, could not possibly expect a commutation. I felt much affected by the fate of Mr. C., on account of his large family, (a wife and ten children) therefore proposed to his eldest daughter, then at Niagara, to accompany me, on behalf of her unfortunate parent; and if we could but get his Lordship to lend an ear to our applications, we need not then fear that the lives of any of the others would be sacrificed, as had been that of the gallant and noble Morrow, who was yet scarce cold in his narrow bed.

Miss C. acceded to my entreaties, provided it would meet the approbation of her father's friends, whom she consulted immediately. They readily assented to the design, and made out the necessary documents. But soon suggested that two appeals might preclude the possibility of either being effective; consequently, it was urged by them, that his Lordship would more likely be struck with the novelty of a daughter asking for the life of her father, than a wife for that of her husband. This was poor reasoning to me, as I could not trust the life of my husband to the pleadings of any but myself; much less to those of an inexperienced girl of eighteen; although I much admired the filial tenderness which led her to make all the efforts she was capable of, to save her father.

An interest was soon excited, and a subscription taken up to bear the expenses of Miss C. to Quebec, with letters of introduction, and so forth; no kindness, at the same time, being extended to me, in whom the project originated, and who had invited Miss C. to accompany me, although I was nearly penniless, which was known, not being near a friend to whom I might apply for assistance; for, indeed, Mr. Wait's nearest friends, who had come to Niagara for the express purpose of aiding me, were induced to withhold even their *countenance*, by the representations made, that if I acted at all, it would rather be prejudicial than advantageous to my husband, on account of my having, also, excited the enmity of the Government. But yet I did not fear being provided for, in an effort of affectionate duty, such as was then before me, and often since has my heart overflowed with gratitude to God, for the sustaining strength given me at that trying period. I was permitted to see my poor husband for one moment, that I might bid him adieu 'ere I left. I endeavored to administer consolation, by encouraging a hope in a happy issue of my suit with Lord Durham, if I could but be permitted to reach him; and commending him to the care of our Heavenly Father, I tore myself from him to embark for Quebec.

I had one more painful duty to perform, before I left Niagara, which was to beg of Dr. Porter, the prison surgeon, that in case my husband should be executed before my return, he would endeavour to prevent that part of the horrid sentence which gave his body to dissection, from being carried into effect, and that his remains might be given to his friends for interment. Dr. Porter assured me, that as far as his influence would extend, I need not fear the reverse; and he, though evidently friendly, thought I had better remain, as he feared the Government might rather be exasperated by an application from me, whose political sentiments they had so clearly understood, from certain letters captured with, and taken from the pockets of Mr. Wait. Still I was not to be deterred from my object; confident in the rectitude of my course, I feared no evil; but passing immediately to the place of embarkation, where I found Miss C., with some of her friends, who were there to see her safe on board. James Boulton, Mr. C.'s attorney, was to accompany her to Toronto, who had taken occasion to use very ungentlemanly language, in his efforts to persuade me not to think of going, for the above reasons, as well as others. I would ruin the cause of his client, and finally prevent the Government from doing anything for the "unhappy prisoners," as he termed them, in mock commiseration; and truly, indeed, would the secret wishes of his unfeeling heart for "those unhappy prisoners," have been realized, had I listened for a moment to their persuasions, and allowed Miss C. to proceed alone, to lay the case at the feet of Lord D.

Here was also Judge BUTLER, *a descendant of the* ROYAL LINE, *of Wyoming notoriety.* He, too, *"felt a deep interest for* the success of the mission, and wondered how a woman, whom, (he had been informed,) manifested a good degree of sense on ordinary occasions, could thus be so *mad-brained* as to persist in exciting the still greater fury of the Government, by personally seeking their mercy, despite of the advice and opinion of all her *friends"* as he pleased to term them. To all of which I had but one reply to make, which was, that the path of duty was before me, from which I would not be driven by any persuasion whatever, and should I have no other friend, I trusted that God would aid me, not only in surmounting the obstacles thus thrown in my way, but finally in accomplishing my purpose. If they thought proper, Miss C. could go in another conveyance, but whether she went or stayed, would make no difference with me.

The bell rang, I stepped on the boat: Mr. Boulton introduced Miss C. to Capt. Richardson, who kindly gave her a passage to Toronto, presented her with four dollars, and a letter of introduction to Capt. Moody, of the St. George; Capt. Richardson not knowing, at the same time, as he told me, on my return, that I was on board of his boat at all, of which, had he been informed, he would most assuredly have been happy in extending the same kindness to me that he had so generously done to Miss Chandler. The St. George was to sail at nine in the morning, for Kingston. We were on board by half past seven, leaving time to reflect on the sad prospect before me, which agonized still more my mind, already on the verge of distraction. I was now about leaving that part of the country where I might hope to meet a friend or acquaintance, who could assist me on the journey of seven hundred miles, undertaken with scarce sufficient means to accomplish it, much less to return 'ere the die might be cast. As these melancholy reflections crowded themselves upon me, the enquiry arose, might I not find some kind friend to humanity in Toronto, before the sailing hour arrived. I resolved at once, went on shore, and requested direction to the residence of Jesse Ketchum, Esq., a gentleman I well knew by reputation, and whom I had once seen at my father's house, on a visit to the lamented Major Randal. I saw Mr. K.—told him my circumstances, and the object of my mission. He introduced me to his interesting and accomplished lady, who kindly insisted on my breakfasting with them, as I could hear the bell there, and reach the boat in time.

Mr. K. read a few verses of consolation from the sacred page. I united with them in their morning worship; and grateful indeed, to my agonized heart, was the privilege of thus pouring out my soul to God in unison with those dear friends, who shed the tear of sympathy with me, and implored the Father of mercies to bestow his gracious blessing. While at breakfast, Mr. K. kindly asked me to accept of ten dollars as an assistant, which I received, as a kindness from heaven. I arose, bade them good morning, and with a heart overflowing with gratitude, proceeded to the boat.

After leaving our moorings, I sent for Capt. Moody, and told him, that as Miss C. and myself were under the necessity of travelling alone, we begged the favour of placing ourselves under his protection. Miss C. presented her letter from Capt. R., which informed him of her peculiar circumstances, and we were both treated with every kindness and attention by the gentlemanly Captain.

On the following morning we arrived at Kingston, and were safely placed on board a small steamer, to descend the St. Lawrence; down which we glided, amid the many picturesque islands, that form a conspicuous feature, in its bewitching scenery, but which, to my anxious heart, could convey scarce one pleasing sensation, absorbed as I was, with feelings of so distressing a nature; though they, together with the pleasing conversation of an interesting family from Philadelphia, who were travelling for pleasure, and were very kind in their attentions, served in a measure to alleviate; and I could look around me with, as I supposed, a species of calmness even wonderful to myself. At the head of the Long Soult, we took the stage to Cornwall; and as it was deemed impracticable to descend the rapids, we were alternately on water and land, until we reached Montreal. I was much struck with the sameness of the quiet little white-washed houses of the French habitans, which seemed only relieved by the occasional residence of the land owner, called the Seniour, and a catholic cross planted in the ground here and there, generally at cross roads. It was in August; and flowers were visible, in great profusion, in and about those humble dwellings; the sash being thrown open, the window sills were filled with blooming geraniums, and other exotic, as well as domestic plants, which at once displayed a most pleasing sight to the travellers, perfumed the atmosphere with their fragrance, and gave evidence of a refined taste in the cultivators of those beauties of nature.

We reached Montreal at eve, and left immediately, per steamboat, for Sorelle, a small village, formerly called William Henry, and situated on the Sorelle river. This place being the residence of Sir John Colbourne, to whose son Miss C. had a letter, asking his influence at Quebec, which she wished to deliver; she requested me to remain there with her until the next boat, to which I acceded, hoping that I also might have an opportunity to obtain the interest of Major Colborne. We accordingly went up to Sir John's. The Major was not at home, but Miss C. left her letter, to call for an answer. I called with her—Major C. came out and gave Miss C. a letter to Col. Couper, the aid-de-camp in waiting, upon the Governor-General. I begged Miss C. to introduce me; but she declined, either from excessive bashfulness, or some other reason unknown to me; consequently I was still left without a line of introduction, recommendation, or any thing, save my own determination to effect the object if possible, let the obstacles be what they might. About nine in the morning we reached Quebec—left our trunks on board, and proceeded immediately to the Castle St. Louis, then the residence of Lord Durham. We enquired the way to the receiving room, and requested to see Col. Couper, who soon made his appearance; upon which Miss C. presented her letter, while I told Col. C. that, although I had not been so fortunate as to bring letters of introduction, yet I had come to memorialize Lord Durham in behalf of a youthful and suffering husband under sentence of death, and hoped that I might be permitted to present my petition to his Lordship. Col. C. thought that the Earl would not be able to see me, as he was suffering from head ache, with other indisposition. He took Miss C.'s petition and waited upon his Lordship, informing me on his return, that the Governor General was then unable to give his attention to the matter, but if I would leave my memorial, Lord D. would consider it, and send the result to my lodgings; to which I replied, that we had but just arrived—as yet had no lodgings, and with his permission, would call for an answer. Ten the following morning was the hour appointed, and we again wended our way to the steam boat.

As we were in a strange city, and knew not where to find a respectable house that might suit circumstances, and hoping to be able to return with the boat the next evening at high tide, I asked the Captain's permission to remain on board, which he readily gave; and as his lady's society enlivened our meals, we were very comfortable, there being a most excellent Stewardess on board. This anxious day and night passed off, and ten in the morning found us again at the Castle, where we were informed by Col. C. that Lord D. in council, had not yet decided on the subject of our memorials; to which I replied, that I most sincerely trusted his Lordship would be pleased to do so that day, as did I not leave Quebec at night with the boat, I could not reach Niagara but to find my husband a mangled corpse; and I had every confidence that Lord D., who had already opened the prison doors in Lower Canada, and set the suffering captives at large, would now extend that clemency in his power, to our friends, and at least spare the lives of those for whom we supplicated. Col. C. hoped we might get an answer by four P.M. and we left to return then; our feelings in the mean time, being more easily conceived than described.

In our way to the wharf, where our asylum was moored, I resolved to make at least a grand effort, that day, to procure the reply, should it not be in readiness at four, although I had no means of doing so but by my entreaties with Col. Couper, unless I could obtain an interview with Mr. Buller, Private Secretary to the Gov. Gen'l which I hoped to do. As I was thus meditating on the subject nearest my heart, and trusting that God in his mercy would overrule all for the best, we were asked by a Canadian who stood near a caleche, if we would like to ride round the city? Yes, was the reply, and thankful was I that any thing had offered to relieve the sad tedium between that hour and four. We rattled through the streets, the principal edifices on which, our good guide described in his best English, and soon drove us to the memorable Plains of Abraham. We stood for a moment on the battle ground where the brave Wolfe and Montcalm had so gallantly yielded up their lives to Him who gave them, and seated ourselves again, were driven, with the permission of the Town Major, to the celebrated Citadel, and found ourselves within the impregnable walls of Cape Diamond, which were lined with artillery and the necessary munitions of war, far surpassing, in strength, any thing I could have conceived of it from description, however minute. We ascended the battery, forming the summit of the immense precipice; and gazed upon the smooth bed of the St. Lawrence lying far beneath, with the beautiful Island of Orleans resting upon its bosom, amid other surrounding scenery equally picturesque. While I contemplated with admiration the union of nature and art, in forming so wonderful and magnificent a fortress, the conversation of a couple of strangers who stood near at once aroused me, as you may suppose, from the subject, to the most painful emotions; for, said one, pointing to a gloomy and dismal part of the Citadel, "there is the prison of those rebels from Upper Canada," naming at the same time, those who were confined there. "At what hour are they allowed to walk?" inquired the other. "At five" was the reply, "they are each permitted to take a half hour's exercise." And must the brave spirits of Canada, thought I, even in this place of undoubted security, be shut from the light of heaven, with the exception of one half hour in the twenty-four, in that earthy abode, (for their prison appeared literally a part of the battery,) and that, too, for the crime of resisting oppression? If in the nineteenth century, and on the western shores of the Atlantic, it must still be considered a crime, by the minions of royalty; Yea, thus it is, and but a few days more will consign my own dear husband to an early grave for the same offence, if mercy stays not the hand of the executioner.

Perceiving, at the close of this painful soliloquy, that the hour of four was drawing near, we resumed our caleche and with palpitating hearts, reached the waiting room at the Castle. Col. C. soon appeared, and was sorry to say he had, as yet, received no communication from Lord D., but still hoped that his Lordship would be enabled to give an answer before the hour for sailing; which Col. C. very kindly offered to send to the boat immediately on the receipt of the same. I begged the favor of an interview with Mr. Buller—Mr. B. was engaged—poor Miss C. sat pale and in tears, while I took the liberty to say that, if Col. C. would permit me, I should esteem it a privilege to sit there until his Lordship was pleased to give a reply—that the time had now arrived when further delay would be adequate to a refusal of Lord D. to grant a commutation; and in that case we could expect to return in time only to embrace the lifeless bodies of those we loved, 'ere they were laid in their tombs; and I *could not* leave that place until his Lordship *did* listen to my entreaties, and spare me the awful alternative. Col. C.'s humane countenance glowed with compassion, he ordered a glass of wine and water for me, and left the room; while with our agitated hearts raised to God, we awaited his return in almost breathless suspense; and thanks to our heavenly Father, we were not long thus to suffer. The *crisis* was passed, as the smiling countenance of Col. C. evinced on his reappearance, when he told us that, although Lord Durham, as Governor General, could not grant a free pardon to our friends without an investigation of their cases, yet he would order a commutation, or at least, stay the execution until the relative documents could be transmitted to him for his own examination; to which effect his Lordship would give us a letter to Sir George Arthur, requesting him to rest for a time, in his sanguinary career; and also, said Col. C.," a special messenger will accompany you with a private despatch to the Lt. Governor." Thus, my dear friend, were the precious lives of our loved ones spared; and we, returning thanks for the kindness and mercy extended, entered our cabins with lighter hearts than we had left them in the morning.

We were in transports when we got under weigh, having already, in imagination, conveyed the happy intelligence to the sufferers; however, we could not so speedily travel in person, and bore the necessary delay as well as possible. On arriving at Montreal, I was informed by the captain, that a Mr. Simpson, M.P. of the Lower Province, who had seen me at Quebec, was on board, and wished an introduction, to which I assented, and recognized, immediately, a gentleman whom I had seen at the Castle St. Louis, engaged in the business of the place. He told me that he resided at Coto-Du-Lac, that he was aware of the object of our mission, and compassionated our distress and loneliness, kindly offering his protection as far as his home; at the same time informing us that Sir George Arthur was then on a visiting tour through that part of the country, and hoped we might meet with him without much delay. Yet the possibility of passing him on the way was indeed cause of much anxiety, but which was repeatedly allayed by the kind enquiries of Mr. S. at every stopping place, assuring us that we had not yet passed him, and indeed a kind providence had willed that we should not. But to return: this gentleman, prompted by the kindness and generosity of his heart, enquired if I had still sufficient means to reach home, and on being informed of the extent of my funds, insisted upon my accepting at least twenty dollars, and assured me that he was most happy to have it in his power to alleviate even that portion of my distress. Again my heart rose in gratitude for this fresh manifestation of the care of Providence, and giving the half of the above kind donation to

Miss Chandler, we felt at ease once more in regard to pecuniary difficulties.

We reached Coto-Du-Lac that evening, where to our inexpressible satisfaction, we found the steamboat that was to convey us to Cornwall waiting for the arrival of Sir George, who was hourly expected. As our kind friend was now to leave us, he gave us his counsel, and we awaited the approach of the Governor, who did not, however, in consequence of some delay, reach there until about eight the following morning, when we soon left our moorings, and giving the messenger time to deliver his despatch from Lord Durham, I made preparations to seek an interview, and wished the captain of the boat to give me an introduction to the Aid in attendance. He accordingly brought Major Arthur, the son of Sir George, whom I informed that I was the bearer of a letter from Lord Durham to the Governor, which I begged the favor of presenting, and hoped he would grant me an interview. The aid left to acquaint his father with the request, and returned saying that the Governor would see us in the ladies' cabin. The captain invited the ladies on deck, leaving us in readiness to receive Sir George, who was soon introduced by the aid.

Sir G., after seating himself, remarked, "You wish to see me, madam." "I do," replied I, "and am happy of the honor, as I have brought a letter from Lord Durham to your Excellency touching cases of vital importance, both to myself and Miss Chandler;" on which I presented the letter, and watched the countenance of the Governor while persuing the same, the dark changes of which indicated no good to our cause if his Excellency could prevent it.

He seemed exceedingly annoyed, and said, "You have appealed to Lord Durham in the case of your husband, under sentence of death for *treason;* and you, for your father," addressing Miss C. "We have," I replied, "and your Excellency will doubtless admit that the importance of the case is a sufficient apology for making any exertion that might be in our power," to which he reluctantly assented, scarce knowing how to express his displeasure, that the victims had indeed been wrested from his deadly grasp, by his superior, who had thus been induced to exert his authority, beyond the limits of Lower Canada. "But, Madam," said he, "I can not accede to the request, and prevent the due course of the law upon offences of this nature." "*You can not accede to the request!* permit me to say, sir, I left Quebec with an assurance from Lord Durham, that the life of my husband should be spared, at least until his Lordship, as *Governor General*, could investigate the matter." "The state of the country, madam demands that examples should be made, and most especially of such *obstinate and henious offenders,*" alluding to Mr. Wait's positive refusal to give any information that would implicate others, which he had sought personally, with an offer of pardon. "And had," said I, "the force of example, as your Excellency is pleased to call those sanguinary measures, and the blood which has already flowed from the gallows, told happily upon the country, I should not now be under the painful necessity of pleading for the life of a beloved husband." "But, madam," he enquiringly remarked, "what am I to do with the repeated applications from the west, imploring me to adopt some measures that may put a stop to those frequent attacks from which Her Majesty's faithful subjects are suffering the loss of life, property, and so forth?" "Permit me to ask your Excellency in return, will the execution of these men restore to the people of the west the lives and property which they have lost by previous aggression?" "By no means," he replied, "but the example may deter others from similar transgressions." "If your Excellency will allow me, I do most sincerely think that no example could go farther to pacify excited feelings, and have a more salutary influence upon the country at large, than a general extension of mercy and pardon to political offenders; for well do I know that the people of this country have been goaded on to rebellion by various and repeated acts of legalized oppression. I crave your Excellency's indulgence, and beg leave to say further, that my friends, even my own family, have been special objects of this oppressive persecution, the effects of which I have felt from my infancy up to this moment; and no longer since than last autumn, my unfortunate husband was told, by several members of the bar, at the Niagara assize, at which he had a suit, that it was useless for him to seek redress, as he was known by the Court to be a *reformer*, and alone, your Excellency, to these sad truths may be attributed the present lamentable state of Canada, a resistance to which has placed my husband in his present melancholy situation. But I fear I am trespassing upon your time, sir, and cannot but trust that your Excellency will view the exciting causes in palliation of the effect, and now follow the beautiful examples of mercy given us in sacred scripture, by kindly allaying the anxiety that agonizes our minds. (He would refer me to the same for consolation)—and I thank God, sir, that a reliance upon sovereign mercy, and confidence in divine Providence, has thus far sustained me under these trying circumstances, and I trust will continue to do so. May we hope that your Excellency will think favourably of our request?"

He could not say that he would, and left the room. Upon which I determined to lay his refusal before Lord Durham by the return of the messenger, who would leave us at Cornwall; consequently begged leave to inform his Lordship, that, although we were assured of the safety of our friends while at Quebec, yet Sir George seemed determined to frustrate his noble purposes of mercy, the benign influence of which I still implored might be extended to Upper Canada, as the Lower Canadians had already, in a measure, felt its radiance. As I was sealing and addressing this communication, the Governor returned, bringing with him Mr. Macaulay, his private secretary, whom he introduced, saying that he had brought his secretary to note down, if we would give it, the substance of the verbal communications we had received in Quebec, which we readily gave, and after which, I told Sir George, that since the honor of his interview, I had taken the liberty of stating the result of the same, with his answer, to Lord Durham, which I intended to forward immediately, holding the letter in my hand. "Oh," said he, "I wish you to understand me, madam, before you communicate my answer to Lord Durham;" and his lip quivered with rage. "And I shall be most happy to understand any thing from your Excellency that may be *aught* more satisfactory than what I have been led to suppose." *"Well, I have granted a respite to your husband, and also to your father,"* addressing Miss C., "but there *must* be more executions, that execrable character, Beemer, must pay the penalty of his act. There shall no mercy be dealt out to him." "Still," replied I, "we must hope that your Excellency will think better of it, and not make another exception to the now happily adopted rule of mercy."

Sir George left us; Mr. Macaulay asked if I was a native of Canada, and being told that I was, he regretted much that I should have been involved in circumstances of so grievous a nature, and hoped that I might be reinstated, and yet be happy in the country of my birth. I thanked him, and he bade us good morning.

We were now nearing Cornwall, where we would land, and where Lord D's messenger would return to Quebec. I considered with what difficulty the acquiescence in Lord D's decision had been extorted from Sir George, who displayed evident symptoms of anger, and entertained fears that he might have been induced by duplicity to stay me with a false hope, that I might not further press the suit with Lord D. I accordingly delivered the letter I had prepared to the messenger, to convey to his master, and could not help feeling a secret satisfaction, that Lord D. would at least be apprised of the apparent disrespect with which the Lieutenant Governor had treated authority; at the same time it being contrary to reason, order, or usage, that he should dare to contravene it. I landed quite indisposed, from mental excitement, and the natural effect of being separated from a nursing babe, on whom, poor little dear, I had scarcely thought since I left. But now that it seemed impossible for her father to fall a victim to the gallows, my feelings naturally recurred to my child, and I feared that she too might be ill; but thank Heaven, I was enabled to cast my care upon Him who is ever the friend of the desolate, and was thus permitted to seek the repose I so much needed. The coach did not leave until morning, when I found myself much refreshed, and better able to pursue my anxious journey.

But to be brief and not weary your patience, I will say little of the latter part of the route; permit me, however, to inform you, that at Prescott we fell in with the Lord Bishop Mountaine, of Montreal, on his way to Toronto; who, clad as he was in his sacerdotal skirt or robe, made rather a singular appearance to those who had never seen a high functionary of the establishment. I was introduced to him, and conversed on the melancholy subject of my mission to Quebec. He was very affable, and kindly pointed me to the great source of consolation under the most trying earthly afflictions. I begged that, if an opportunity offered of his aiding me with his influence at Toronto, he would give it; which he said was a difficult matter with a person standing in the relation to the Crown that he did; but that he might have an opportunity of benefitting my cause, which he would be glad to embrace, as he deeply commiserated my painful situation.

The good Bishop left us at Toronto, our anxiety seemingly increasing with every revolution of the wheels, until we reached Niagara, where we landed on the 22d, and found preparations making for the execution of our friends on the approaching 25th. We flew to the prison to communicate the happy intelligence of the promised respite; but having nothing official with us, and no orders to that effect having as yet been sent, our report of mercy was scarcely credited; indeed, the jailer had received orders from the Sheriff to have all things in readiness to carry out the horrid sentence to the letter. I saw my dear husband for a moment, and endeavoured to console him by assurances that the respite would come, as I had it from both Lord Durham and Sir George, who *could* not thus practice deception. He informed me that our dear child had been dangerously ill, though at the last accounts from her she was rather better. Still I could not see her, she being twenty miles distant, and I on the following morning must retrace my steps to Toronto, and learn the reason why the expected respite had not been sent. Accordingly, at eight in the morning I again left the wharf for Toronto, scarce knowing to whom I might apply in the absence of the Governor, whom I had left at Cornwall; but was determined on finding some of the officials. I stepped into a carriage and told the lad to drive to the residence of the Chief Justice—he did so—the house was shut up. Drive to the Solicitor General's, said I, but seeing a gentleman in the way I asked the boy if he knew him. Yes, replied he, it is Judge McLean; upon which I stopped, and asked the gentleman if I had the honor of addressing Judge McLean? He replied in the affirmative, when I told him the importance of my errand, and begged that he would inform me where I might find the members of the executive council. He very kindly directed me to the Parliament House, where the council were then sitting, and to which he said he was going. On reaching the place I was shown to Mr. Sullivan, of whom I begged leave to enquire whether the Governor had not ordered a respite for the Niagara prisoners? at the same time informing him what I had been told at Quebec, as well as what Sir George had himself said, a few days previous, in the presence of Mr. Macaulay and Miss Chandler. To which he replied, that he had as yet received no such communication from his Excellency, but should there be reality in the matter, we might expect the respite over per the Transit on the following morning at eleven o'clock; and if I had it from the Governor, he said I might of course rely upon it: still I felt misgivings on the subject; and the possibility of its being a ruse of Sir George, the better to carry out his predetermined purposes of cruelty, would force itself upon me notwithstanding the many reasons I had to expect the reverse. I accordingly called on Bishop Mountaine—informed him of my fears and hopes, and entreated him to see the council, and advise them to stay proceedings until something did arrive from Sir George. He promised to do what he could. I had now but time to reach the steamboat, which was ringing for the last call, and I hurried on board, to await the anxious time near my husband, whom I could not see that night, it being six when we arrived. Yet I was enabled to trust in God, and beseech Him who could turn the hearts of men to mercy, and rule all events for our good and His glory, to smile upon us in this our time of trial, and grant us sustaining grace to await His will.

This night passed, and in the morning, though not knowing but the worst might come, I endeavoured to encourage my husband, when permitted to hand in his breakfast through the irons bars that separated us, in the hope of the respite being over at eleven that day; but this hope was doomed to disappointment. I thought the evening boat must be the bearer of it; still it came not at six, and the next day, between the hours of eleven and one, was the time appointed for the executions. Yet I could not help but feel that come it must and would, though nearly distracted by this cruel delay of the Governor, who evidently, at the best was determined to torture us literally the last moment. My hopes were now centered in the arrival of the Transit at eleven, which came, but brought not the message of mercy; neither did she bring the expected Sheriff, who had gone to Kingston with those prisoners who had been deemed more worthy of a commutation by Sir George; and as a last hope, the possibility of his bringing the order from the Governor at Kingston or of being absent until after the allotted time had arrived of the Government steamer bringing the Sheriff, who was indeed the bearer of the long expected respite fresh from the hand of Sir George Arthur, whom he had left the day before at Kingston.

I must leave you to imagine this overwhelming scene, as I cannot even attempt to describe it, or give you the least idea of the feelings, caused by the safety of four precious lives thus spared by a merciful God, who had deigned to hear and answer our prayers; and will close this lengthy epistle by informing you, that, as soon as the violence of those feelings had in measure subsided and our hearts had been raised in gratitude to the Most High for this wonderful deliverance, I left Niagara, and hastened to embrace my dear babe, who was with her grandmother, and whose health I found on my arrival, was so much improved that I was enabled to remove her on a pillow the following day to Niagara, that I might still be convenient to her suffering father, near whom I remained until the subsequent order for his removal to Fort Henry, at Kingston.

Yours, most respectfully,
Maria Wait.

4

Transportation in Lieu of Death

Ashgrove, near Oatlands, V.D.L.
June, 1840.

To ——,

Dear Sir: The arrival of the respite though for so brief a period, burst like a meteor upon our minds, and gave us not "a faint glimmering hope," but a positive assurance of an effective interposition; for when once a delay was obtained, and the documents lodged in the hands of the Earl of Durham, there could be no doubt of a lenient course being pursued, and no more blood be spilled in this case; for the application made in behalf of myself and Mr. Chandler would equally benefit the others, who were reserved with *us* for execution. The interposition of the Earl in the affairs of U.C. called forth some harsh censures from Sir George Arthur, and it led to serious altercations between the two dignitaries. Sir G. in his private despatches to his Lordship, remonstrated "in no measured terms," against his having been induced "to listen to the appeals of a wife and a daughter of two of the most aggravated offenders, and interpose between them and the just execution of the law." The recent publication of the official documents bearing on this point, are conclusive evidence; that to these personal petitions alone, can we attribute the preservation of our lives. This respite was soon followed by another of ten days, and subsequently one of near a month, extending the time to the first of October, when the deputy Sheriff appeared at the jail, bearing in his hand a letter, ostensibly from the Lieutenant Governor, with orders for him to read it to us, and receive and transmit our answers. It informed us that "His Excellency, in council, had concluded to listen to our petitions and grant pardons, on condition of our accepting transportation in the lieu of death." Of course transportation as an alternative, was generally preferred, and answers were given accordingly—yet not on my part without a counter "condition" —for I supposed it a mere mockery, to give coloring to his unbending arrogance, not once giving him credit for the full share of superciliousness his subsequent conduct proved him to possess in so great a degree; and consequently replied that, "if by transportation, he meant only to convey me from Niagara, or even to England, I should not oppose it; but would prefer death to being banished to Van Dieman's Land, therefore would not accept the terms of the pardon." Although I gave a conditional answer, yet I did not perceive the extent of this artifice, or that it would be made a subterfuge for law. But in England I found much importance attached to that condition, for it was assumed by the ministry, as ground sufficient for carrying the "commuted sentence" into full effect.

A few days after this "compact" arrangement, the clanking of chains announced an intended removal. When the execrable fetters were riveted on my limbs, the cautering iron entered my soul; and not till then did I feel, I was truly no longer free; *a manacled slave* was a conception I never before rightly understood. I had not valued personal liberty as I ought, but now that was for ever gone, I viewed it as the most precious boon Heaven could bestow. All the wealth of the world was as nothing in comparison to it; and on the contrary, slavery was the most abhorrent of all evils.

Mrs. Wait as usual, was now at hand to offer condolence, and calm my perturbed feelings. She packed up what clothes I had there, and forgot not the few books, a perusal of which had given me pleasure. She awaited with resignation far superior to mine, the fiat that should separate our persons perhaps for ever. I kissed and caressed that dear, dear child, you speak so tenderly of, and wrung the hand of her whose affectionate care I fancied I was no more to experience. This was a scene I had often anticipated, and thought myself prepared to meet; but I had looked upon it superficially, and seen it only in the distance. A sense of desolation came over me that I could not shake off; and had it not been for the superior fortitude taught me by Mrs. Wait, I fear I should have shown a feminine spirit—a want of manhood. We had but little time for leave-taking—were torn from mourning friends and hurried on board a steamer for Toronto, where we arrived at the dusk of the evening, on the 6th October. We found an immense multitude crowding the wharf, and lining the street through which we were to pass to the jail. From them proceeded mingled shouts of imprecations and pity—derision and sympathy. But I soon observed it was by the squalid alone that imprecations were uttered, while compassion was visible in the countenances of all who appeared worthy respect. It is true, such salutations, at first discomposed my mind a little, but the commiseration of the better class reconciled me to this new species of greeting, and I felt that I should ever prefer the insult to the praise of the varying mob

At the jail we were received by the very *obsequious host* Mr. Kid, who invited us to walk into the hall, *humanely* offering the dirty floor for a lodging We could not, of course, return him much a compliment for his *generosity* Nothing was offered here to eat, and we should have been obliged to go supperless to bed, had not the guard kindly shared their provisions with us on board, before reaching Toronto. In this respect we have already found the common soldier generous, even beyond his means. This was the first night I had essayed to rest with my leg and wrist coupled to another and I found the attempt nugatory. Here too, I first found vermin, i.e. fleas and bugs, which crept into our clothes, and in the morning refused to part company. After rising, a draught from a milk woman's pail did more to revive drowsy nature, than would a dozen pots of Mr. Kid's ale, which he profusely offered, "provided always," we would first present him with the "proper equivalent." Our escort, with Wheeler at their head, arrived very early, and led us to the dock, through the same scenes we had witnessed the evening previous. We put off at eight, and reached Kingston by the following dawn, when we were immediately marched away to the jail, a large edifice near the center of the town, where we remained seated on the floor, until twelve M., when we were again called on to move. At this time a waggon was provided for us, in which we were driven slowly across the Rideau to Fort Henry, followed and accompanied by the Kingston Sheriff, deputy, and jailer, the Niagara deputy and jailer, with a whole division of red coats, carrying arms at present. At the gates of the fort the guard was turned out to receive us and our entrance was between two platoons of soldiers, which closed after us as if to shut out the hope of ever repassing that barrier. Fort H. is constructed of good workmanship, on a commanding position, and has an imposing appearance. It is commodiously planned, and has an area of about a half acre, with a large reservoir for water underneath. If well manned, it might hold out against almost any number of assailants.

Our irons were soon knocked off, and our pockets searched—money, knives and papers taken from us, but afterwards, all but the papers were restored. The prisoners already here, consisting of those from Toronto, London District Point au Pelee, and Niagara, were in two rooms or wards, without communication.

I was, with three others, McLeod, Beemer, and Warner, ushered into the one occupied by Messrs. Parker, Wixon, Watson, and fifteen or sixteen others, where we found a breakfast prepared, of which we partook with avidity, it being the first food offered that day, though then near four P.M. I was surprised, and even piqued, by the congratulations with which I was greeted by all. It seemed a perfect verifying of the old sentiment of "misery likes company." But I soon discovered that it was a genuine burst of joy for our opportune escape from death; for of our respite and ultimate commutation, they had received no information previous to that morning, and necessarily supposed we had suffered the penalty designed.

As soon as I had time to look about me and make inquiry, I found my companions consisted of what remained of the Toronto, London District prisoners, and J.G. Parker, while the others occupied a ward adjoining. Parker and Watson were the two unfortunately recaptured after the celebrated escape of sixteen persons from this fort—fourteen of whom succeeded in reaching the U.S. I obtained a circumstantial account of the whole affair, but do not consider it necessary to be given here. I looked upon it as a daring adventure, that must have emanated from a fearless, intrepid spirit, and been guided by a master hand, that would have done honor to the cause of liberty, if brought into full action in the field of battle. The whole exhibits a sagacity and courage belonging to but few, who were left to act in the patriot cause. We can only conjecture what the effect would have been, had these and other restrained brave spirits had a proper field for action. It will remain a wonder to all who visit the fort, how a plan participated in by so many, could have been matured and followed up with sufficient precaution, to permit the digging through a four foot wall, and traversing of near half the underground rooms and outside trench of the fort, with success. While we were there many persons visited the interior, with no other motive than to witness the theatre of so noted an escape, from such an impregnable fortress.

I found the society very agreeable indeed; and our time was not "killed," as is usually the case with prisoners, nor spent in games of chance, swearing, lewd conversation, tale-telling, &c. &c. But industry prevailed—all were engaged in something useful, ornamental or entertaining—some were reading, some writing; others were occupied in making port folios, small wooden boxes, or other mementoes for friendly presents. I soon introduced the art of making a sort of curiously wrought paper memorial, on which were inscribed, in elegant style, names and short pithy motoes, savoring of patriotism and philanthropy. These were eagerly sought after, and bundles of them were sent to our friends every opportunity.

Messrs. Wixon, Watson, Tidey, Parker, McLeod, and myself united in an association, soon after we had come among them, for the purpose of literary improvement and amusement for the long evenings, by delivering, in rotation, original lectures. In writing, delivering, or listening to them, the time rolled cheerfully and unheeded on.

My first address was upon the subject of Patriotism. I spoke ardent and earnestly, and with all the ability and eloquence I was master of; for it was a subject that had actuated every nerve of my system, and reduced me to my present slavish situation. By request, I copied it for several persons, among whom was Mr. Parker, whose copy fell into the hands of the tory faction at Cornwall, and became the cause of considerable harshness, for it spoke very disparagingly of the government.

Every Sabbath we listened with pleasure to an evangelical discourse and instructing commentations on the Psalm of David, with other interesting passages of scripture, by Mr. Wixon. Indeed, we had great reason to regard the presence of this very excellent man as contributing largely to our spiritual good and temporal quiet. About two weeks after our arrival, Sir George Arthur visited the fort. He made his *entre* with as much pomp and parade as the head of all the Autocrats would assume on a gala day. After an array and manouvering of all the soldiers in the garrison, he took possession of one of the officers rooms, and sent for most of the prisoners, particularly those from Niagara. But I was slighted. There was no condescension, no courtesy for me. I had displeased him, unpardonably offended him, and he must show it. Since the Earl of D. had resigned, and left the government in the charge of Sir John Colborne, a man equally bloodthirsty as himself, he felt no restraint, and no disposition to mollify, but to add to the mental misery of all who were under his displeasure. While he had given hope to all called upon, for a lenient course being pursued in each individual case, and an admission to freedom on guaranteed good conduct, "there was no favor to be expected by the obstinate Wait." Our provisions consisted of one pound of bread, three-fourths pound fresh meat, and a small quantity of vegetables served us twice per week—tea and sugar we supplied ourselves. The food was prepared by one of our number, sent to a hireling for cooking, and invariably returned short of what it went out. The bread seldom lasted the time it was designed; and I have known eighteen extra loaves bought in our ward in one week, in addition to the rations received.

The prisoners apartments were visited every day by the Sheriff, deputy, with two or three, and sometimes six or eight, military officers, accompanied by a sergeant, corporal, and file of men, to guard the entrance, while the room underwent a critical examination by the civil, in presence of the military functionaries. Every bed, box or package was removed, so that each square inch of the floor could be seen and sounded; Clothes hanging against the wall, were carefully moved aside, that no spot might be hid from view. The men likewise were all paraded in the middle of the ward, in single file, and answered to their names, while the sergeant audibly counted the number present, and an ensign referred to a paper held in his hand, to see that none were missing. In joking a Captain who visited, relative to the extreme precautions used, he replied—"you Yankees are such slippery fellows, that we never know when we've got you. Stone walls, iron grates, and *red coats* are no security." They were warned to these daily examinations by the late escape.

We usually had a man stationed at the window about the hour of the customary visits, to report the approach of the officers, when every article of amusement or memento would be put aside; for an order had been issued by the commandant, prohibiting the manufacture of those trifles, fearing they had been, or would be, used as bribes for the sentinel, &c. On the morning of the fourth of November the man at the window reported the approach of the sheriff, accompanied by two females. My heart fluttered with intense anxiety, while I thrust my face among the dozen the report had brought to the grate, to catch a glimpse of the individuals mentioned, each hoping to discover in them a friend. As soon as I caught a view of the figures, the expression of "my wife" burst from my lips in deep pathos. In an inordinate tremor of delight, I waited the tardy unlocking of the door, when I found in my embrace the object of all my anxious solicitude but a shadow of mortality. In every lineament of the face were visible traces of care and intense anxiety. Unusual exertion, combined with deep mental distress, had made sad havoc of youth and of health, though the spirit was yet whole and the mind still firm.

This new expression of her affection, despite the dangers of late lake navigation, endeared her more, if possible, to my heart than ever, and I felt, though a prisoner, I would not exchange conditions with the man, though wealthy and free, who had no affection lavished upon him but what his riches purchased. We had but a few minutes for conversation. The sheriff, as soon as he had examined the room, told her to leave, as he must lock the door. However, she stood awhile at the grated window, but not a word must pass without being heard by the guard, or a trifle given without examination. A parcel containing winter clothes, a few pounds of tea, some butter and dried fruit, with a pail of preserves, were cautiously inspected before they could be given up to me. The same conduct was pursued towards Miss Chandler in her communications with her father, in the next ward. Mrs. Wait visited me each morning while I remained, for the sad consolation of fifteen minutes conversation at the window, for subsequent to the first visit she was debarred entering the door.

At that time, my health was very good, not having indulged in useless repining, but drawing my mind as much as possible from all sources of discontent and sorrow, having been taught, that contentment in a calm and quiet mind, is a "bank that never fails; a bank that yields a perpetual dividend of happiness," let the possessor be in whatever situation he may, a prison, a work-house, or poverty at home. And, that industry was a virtue that would take away half the dreariness of the prison walls. It does, indeed, busy the mind, and thus prevent the gathering of gloom, while it raises pleasures by exercising the fancy; and imparts delight by the development of heretofore hidden faculties or abilities. When at large, amid the quiet and pleasant "flowery fields," one must be of a very lethargic disposition indeed, who could not enjoy the prospect, and indulge in the pleasures of life: but when he is incarcerated, and all the beauties of nature, the feelings, sympathies, and publications of the world and society are shut from him, if his mind can associate the pictured fancies of the landscape with objects, however gloomy, around him, and feel thankful for thus much of enjoyment, he is truly worthy of happiness. While here in this fort, Beemer gave the first indication of a deceitful and treacherous disposition. It was observed by some of our companions, yet I could not receive the opinion. But few of the number, however, would associate with him, on account of his extreme vulgarity and obscene conversation. During the hour permitted for daily recreation in the area of the fort, a small space of which was allotted to us, Beemer would walk to and fro, dark and moodily, in appearance a perfect personification of one of Milton's "fallen angels, devising nefarious schemes against the human race." I believe, however, his feigned disclosures gained no favor at the *"fount of law,"* though penned by the inimitable John Arthur Tidey.

For some time after our arrival, rumors were afloat of the Governor sending part of our number to Quebec; and when his Excellency visited the fort, it was said by some that they had been informed by him, a part of the prisoners should be freed on bail, while others would be sent to Quebec. But these reports had died away, and we began to suppose the lateness of the season precluded the possibility of a removal. But on the morning of the 9th of November, we were miserably undeceived upon that subject, for much earlier than usual, Sheriff McDonald entered the fort, accompanied by Mrs. Wait. He came directly to our ward, and announced the order of the Governor for an "immediate removal to Quebec, for safe keeping during the winter, of Wixon, Watson, Parker, Wait, McLeod, Chandler, Walker, Alves, Bedford, Malcolm, Brown, Anderson, Waggoner, Vernon, Miller, Reynolds, Grant, Mallory, Gemmell, McNulty, Cooley, Van Camp and Beemer. The others, Tidey, Hart, &c., will remain for further orders." He continued, "the orders are peremptory for an immediate march, for he does not think it safe to retain you here, as the country is in a state of excitement and alarm, in the expectation of an irruption from the States. You will, therefore, have but an hour to prepare in, which you will, of course, use to best advantage. Wait, if he wishes, can accompany his wife to one of the vacant rooms where they will be out of the bustle, and my deputy will attend them, with an armed guard, and particularly observe that no papers or other illicit articles pass between them unexamined." We accepted the offer of the sheriff as a courtesy, and followed the deputy to a room only occupied by the trunks, clothes, baggage, &c., of Messrs. Montgomery, Brophe, &c., left in their flight, while we in turn were closely followed by a red coat, who in his heart pitied our forlorn prospect, but dare not show it in presence of the unfeeling civic menial. Soon after we entered, Mrs. Wait endeavored to put in my hand unobserved some papers she had written since arriving at Kingston, for her own pastime and my amusement, but the hawk eye of the servile lackey quickly detected the act, when they must, of course, be submitted to his perusal before given up to me. And I am sure every word was duly scanned, as if he feared some treason lurked in the letters, for during the perusal, he was several times obliged to refer to the writer for elucidation. Such ungenerous conduct elicited an audible groan of disgust from the breast of the sentry. The deputy was called away for a few moments, and the soldier showed his liberality by turning his back, as if to say, "now, do as you please;" and well were those few moments improved, for a hasty exchange of papers and mementoes took place, and when the deputy returned, there was no need of his vigilance.

We had a great deal to say to each other, but as we were in a few minutes to separate, perhaps forever, our time was spent in encouraging each other by pointing the mind and hope to Him who will watch over all who trust to his unerring counsel; though we were cast upon the wide world without other hope, He would be to us a guide and surety against despair; though the enemy taunt and oppress, He would be merciful and lenient. In conjecturing my probable destination and ultimate fate, I mentioned the likelihood of being sent to England whither, she declared she would follow, if by any means it could be accomplished; and she was sure her personal appeals there, would result in my freedom. The idea of the voyage across the ocean, by a female, alone and unprotected, and the obstacles she would have to surmount, with the probability of meeting an unsympathising and unfriendly feeling in London, made me shudder and repudiate the *thought*. But her mind, her heart, her all, were enlisted; and she promptly directed me to her success, through every embarrassing circumstance, in her former appeals to the Earl of Durham. But I still urged the difference between an inland journey of fourteen hundred miles, surrounded with known sympathy; and a voyage across the wide ocean, unprotected, amid strangers whose kindness would be doubtful. She would point me to Him who sustains the feeble, guards the way-worn, and protects the friendless in every trial of danger, and every vicissitude of fortune. As a last argument to deter her from the resolution she had expressed, I mentioned our dear babe, whom she ought now to consider as the only link that bound her affections to earth. *That*, indeed, was a subject that vibrated every chord in her nature, and, as I fancied, for a moment, made her swerve; but it was only for a moment, and that, too, was met by the same undaunted reliance on Providence; and with a countenance radiant with superior fortitude, she said, "will not He who tempers the wind to the shorn lamb, and as a shepherd carries them in His bosom, keep her from neglect and want? Yes: should I hear of your removal to Van Dieman's Land, and be unsuccessful in my petitions to the Queen, I *will* follow you thither, and share your exile, nothing loth in leaving our child in the hands of the 'orphan's God'." I was effectually silenced; yet had I desired to offer any further impediments, they would have been that instant cut short, by a summons to come and be invested with the chains of honor. Our minds had been wrought up, not to the climax of despair, but to a high hope and ardent buoyancy; and we snatched a hasty adieu with a calmness that I often wonder at. Oh that I could ever be guided, or actuated, by the same inspiring feelings of resignation that were infused in my soul at that last parting scene. Not one murmur was breathed against my wayward destiny, but my heart was filled with an inexpressible glow of satisfaction; *that* continued to cheer, and buoy it up, until the last farewell wave of the handkerchief of my bosom companion died in the distance, and I found myself on the bow deck of a steamboat, coupled hand and foot to J.G. Parker, and surrounded with my companions in tribulation, among a number of horses, who disputed possession with us, as well as a whole regiment of regulars, whose bristling bayonets showed well that no escape from there was practicable. As a new scene is now commencing, I will close this communication.

I remain, dear sir,
Yours, &c. &c.

5

KINGSTON TO MONTREAL

Ashgrove, near Oatlands, V.D.L.
August 1840.

To ——,

My Dear Sir: My last closed on the 9th of Nov., at the embarkation of twenty-three state prisoners on board the steamer Coburgh, and the last parting scene with my wife. When the fiat went forth that separated us, probably forever, she followed at a distance, (as near as the humanity of our guards would permit her to approach,) saw my legs and arms shackled, and still accompanied to the place of embarkation, and there stood in the face of a chill wintry wind, waving adieus until we were lost to her sight.

When aroused to a sense of reality by the surrounding objects of life, and the pains caused by the chains of despotism, I began to give place to a conception of loneliness, and a disposition to review the chequered scenes of the past, or to pierce the dark veil of futurity that hung like a pall before me. Neither hope nor calmness forsook me; I felt that every principle actuating my heart, and inducing me to take the part I did in opposition to oppression, was founded on truth, on justice, and on philanthropy; and necessarily the exertions must ultimately result to the good of some, although there was no probability of my participating in that good, yet the anticipation carried with it a full compensation for all my personal suffering and loss. I could see in the obscurity of the future a succession of trials, of distress, and of sorrow; yet beyond was a gleam of sunshine, a bright halo of joy, piercing the gloom, and beaconing me on to the rencounter, with not a mere hope, but a glowing confidence, grounded on substantial evidence, that has not yet deserted me, though a gulf of sorrow and banks of trouble must yet be traversed ere I reach the gleam of sunshine, or am encircled by that halo of joy; the partaker of freedom reunited to the dear ones of earth. Still the probability of evil and want befalling those loved ones, occasionally brought with it a corroding thought, a bitter pang, yet God was their shield, in whom they trusted, and surely I ought not to mourn distresses I knew no certainty of.

Our quarters on board the steamer were most uncomfortable, crowded on the bow deck, and penned in on all sides by the military guard, with three horses among us, and the deck covered with their litter, upon which we must either lie or stand, while the weather was very cold, and we had nothing but our own clothes to protect us from it. The horses were restive, and often endangered the lives and limbs of those who essayed to find a bed near them. Our baggage had been piled on our inner skirt; Parker and myself availed ourselves of its contiguity, and settled down upon it, where I endeavored to lull myself to sleep, but vainly, for whenever I fell into a drowse, the piercing cold communicated by the iron on my bare wrists, would suddenly arouse me to painful sensations; and the chains upon my leg kept that in a state of numbness. Yet these were not evidences sufficient to remind us of our debasement.

The comfort of sitting was too much for us to enjoy in the presence of a stripling ensign of the 93d regiment of the Queen's Own L.I. who happened to pass and observed us. He instantly ordered the sentry to "prick up the d-d rebels with his bayonet, and make them stand." We regarded not the order, supposing it given only in the exuberance of violent spirits; but this petty officer, early schooled in the brutal policy of his government, enraged at the slight his authority had suffered, drew his sword, and swore he "would force up the villains, and send them forward among the herd." But I could not discern the necessity of resigning my seat and standing, during a cold and tedious night, therefore remained unmoved. This obstinacy created an altercation that brought to the deck Commander Major Arthur, who, before any enquiry, gave the usual order to "shoot down the prisoners if any suspicious movements were observed;" and then demanded "the cause of the row." The officer replied "it was (my) refusal to obey his orders and move forward." "Does he!" returned the redoubted Arthur, "I wish I was empowered to do so, I would rid the world of them all at once, and thus relieve the British government of further trouble with them."

The master of the boat came to his assistance, with language more fitting a Billingsgate Calender than this letter, of which Parker got his full share. I still remained sitting, and pointed out the impossibility of finding room, even for standing, forward of where we were, when the civic officer, in whose immediate charge we were placed, interfered, and begged we might be suffered to remain. It was "granted," and the valiant Major, with his Billingsgate champion, returned to their cabin and their cups. The mystery was explained by the sentry, "on the sly," who said, "you should have arisen when the officer ordered it, and then you could have sat down again, and nothing more would have been said. He only wanted to show his authority." Well! well! thought I, if we must receive such marks of the power of every petty minion we meet, our *restraint* will not be *pleasant*.

We glided down the waters of the Ontario and St. Lawrence with speed, and found ourselves at a wharf at Prescott very early the following morning. Here lay the small steamboat Dolphin, with a piece of brass ordinance mounted on her bow, and a company of volunteers on board. About eight we were transfered to her, and prepared to descend the Long Sault rapids. The morning was extremely cold, and we suffered much, being entirely unsheltered. The day, however, became fine as the sun approached the meridian, and we enjoyed with considerable delight the passage down this noble river, though the novelty was interrupted by the clinking of chains, and the pains from our wristlets. As we approached the head of the Long Sault, we beheld the river narrowing to a very contracted channel, down which "the waters of many lakes" whirled with a dizzying rapidity that seemed to betoken destruction to our frail bark. "Its war of waters tumultuous roar," and the giddy whirl of its eddies, appeared to yawn in terror upon us, and the master and crew were palsied with fear, for this was the first attempt at "riding the Sault" with a craft of that kind, and only risked through the imperious necessity of a passage boat below, to replace one scuttled and sunk by the patriots.

However, we "threaded the passage" safely, rounded to at the foot to wood, and then continued to Cornwall, where we arrived about two P.M., having accomplished the distance in an incredible short space of time. It was said then, that the distance of nine miles was run in fifteen minutes. In passing down the St. Lawrence, the rumor of excitement was verified by multitudes of militia collected and drilled upon its banks, who generally saluted us with loud huzzas, roused, probably, by the cannon on our deck. We passed unanswering, save in one solitary case, when Mr. J.J. McNulty (the poor fellow is now dead) sprang upon the cannon, dragging his boon companion with him, and shouted three times, in a stentorian voice, "Hurra for the Patriots!" then leaped down amid the deafening "bravos" of his companions. We nearly paid dear for his temerity, for the sound of "Patriots," brought the mushroom gentry's arms to a present, but perhaps their guns were charged with something besides powder, or had "wooden flints" in them, for nothing followed. The whole lines we passed evidently expected a descent, for when our boat, carrying no ensign, rounded to from the American channel of the Long Sault, or approached near the shores, the banded militia fled in evident panic or skulked to watch the movements of the boat.

The rain commenced falling in torrents just before we reached Cornwall, to which we were exposed without remedy. As soon as we touched the wharf, the commandant of the station, Col. Turner, (who sported a Waterloo Sergeant's Medal on the outside breast of his coat,) was, with his officers, called to hold a council in the cabin of the boat, which, after an hour spent in consultation, determined on detaining us there for a few days, until the "rising below should be quelled," which *we* hoped would succeed to the hearts content of the participators, and visit Cornwall ere many hours. Col. Turner's corps were turned out in the rain to guard us to the jail, who were a set of as ragged, and as hideous looking wretches as I ever beheld in the shape of men.

When they were ranked in double file, the gallant colonel from under the awning of the boat, ordered them to "load with ball cartridge, and shoot down every man who showed the slightest disposition to escape." Our luggage was thrown upon the deck, that the boat might be used to carry men to the scene on the other shore, of the "high spirited war" that was being waged against defenceless women and children, and the conflagration of their houses, barns and stores. When all were prepared for marching, and the colonel on horseback, he took the opportunity of haranguing his "noble fellows," in the true spirit of an upstart British swaggart, with no other apparent design than to impress us with high ideas of his consequence, and keep us longer exposed to the pitiless storm. I am sure he could not have taken a course better calculated to exemplify a mean cowardly heart, than the one he adopted. And not a man among us gave him credit for any thing more than what he really was worth. There is no conceiving how long we might have been subjected to this detention, had not the rain cooled his garrulity, and benefitted us by producing the order to "march."

The road was uncommonly bad, and it was with exertions painful in the extreme, that we drew our chained limbs along, encumbered with a part of our baggage, which we were told we must carry or lose; the remainder, however, was subsequently sent after us. We finally reached the jail, a large brick building, three quarters of a mile from the landing, with an imposing appearance upon the outside. But inside, like the Jewish sepulchres, "filled with dead men's bones," alias, filth, vermin, and a number of the drunken orange soldiery, thrown in the cells for a few hours, to give time for their superabundant spirits to evaporate. Indeed, a shelter of any kind, would have been, at that time, peculiarly grateful; so when we were ushered into the large dirty hall, we were not disposed to murmur at the absence of all comfort, a "roaring fire excepted," which soon, however made us feel the consequences of a sudden transition from severe cold to intense heat. The badness of the roads, and inclemency of the weather, had fatigued us so effectually, that we were fain to throw ourselves upon the floor, as soon as we entered. Our clothes, saturated with rain, steaming in the heat, rendered our condition horribly disagreeable; and the iron clevies upon our wrists had also caused them to swell in such a manner, that on some the iron was buried in the flesh, causing excrutiating pain, as well the inconvenience of retaining upon us our upper garments. You can scarce form an idea of our circumstances; mine were as follows—In the first place, I had on a cloak with my manacled arm through the arm hole; then an over and an under coat, all of which I had thrown off as far as I could, leaving them hanging on my right arm. Parker had done the same with two coats, thus we had four wet coats and a cloak dangling between us, no slight inconvenience, you will say, for persons fatigued as we were. We felt it so; indeed, we thought it unendurable, and applied to some young officers, who out of curiosity visited us during the night, to have the cuffs removed. They brought the colonel to see us, but instead of his sympathy being excited by our sufferings, he swore he would add to, rather than diminish our irons, or decrease our "deserved punishments."

I felt enraged at his inhumanity, and declared, if my life was spared, and liberty regained, I would meet him again, when he would dearly rue his brutality to defenceless prisoners. He muttered curses upon my insolence, and departed. Nothing daunted, we next sent for the military surgeon, who came, examined our wrists, and said "it was indeed too bad," but he had no power to act, further than to advise a release from the cuffs, which he did, without effect. And we poor slaves of caprice must spend the night with all our wet clothes and irons on, upon the floor, without bed or bedding, rest or sleep. A cup of tea from the provident store of Mrs. Wait, revived drooping nature a little. Indeed, it was with a blessing upon her head that we partook of it at this time, and subsequently; on the morning following, a very good breakfast, of beef steak and tea, was furnished by the good natured Dutch jailer, who, while we were eating, entertained us with some of his complaints against the government. He said his father had been ruined by the government, and so had himself; still he thought he ought to be loyal. About eleven, the Deputy Sheriff who accompanied us from Kingston, made his appearance, for the first time since landing, offering the inclemency of the weather as an excuse, forgetting our greater inconvenience in the mean time. After he had examined our wrists, he concluded to take the cuffs off for the day; but a "rumor of invasion" came while he was in the act; he therefore reinvested us with them immediately, permitting us, however, to throw off our upper garments, and have them put on transversly, viz., my left hand to Mr. P's right, while my right leg was chained to his left. Thus we remained for two days, cross ironed; yet it was a relief to the arm first invested. We therefore spent the day in comparative comfort, and enjoyed a season of refreshing prayer, with scriptural reading and a religious discourse, by Mr. Wixon, who, having but one leg, was not encumbered with irons.

The town of Cornwall, and, indeed, every part of the country, was in a state of fearful alarm and excitement. Terror was depicted in every countenance we saw—Turner's was not excepted. We were rigidly guarded, and every motion was observed; pens, ink and paper were taken fearing we might give information of our detention there and a consequent rescue be attempted. Various rumors were hourly arriving, of the Patriot's success, magnified, of course, by the credulous relater. The reports were not destined for our ears; but the proximity of the council chamber, and the earnest trepidation with which the news was related, rendered it impossible for a word to escape our hearing; consequently the exaggerated accounts raised our anticipations and hopes to high expectations.

On the second day of our continuance at Cornwall, the steamboat returned with a load of volunteers; and two hundred stand of arms were distributed to them from the door of the jail. These additional men, it was expected, would effectually secure the place against the expected attack; yet the officers who gave out the arms, expressed fears, in a consultation, of these very guns being turned against themselves. Indeed, I believe if the place had been attacked by a very few resolute men, not only would it have been carried, but nearly all the militia would have become insurgents.

On Monday, a number of the young militia officers visited us, and were very communicative; they repeatedly intimated a hope, nay, an assurance, that we would not be retained as prisoners much longer. Our cuffs were removed for a few hours during the day; but, out of *compassion,* were locked on for the night. We laid down early, in our clothes; and the orders were strict against having any lights burning in the jail that night, fearing they might operate as beacons, to the attacking party. About ten an alarm was sounded, and we, the poor slaves of caprice and terror, were ordered for removal instantly. But before we could get on our overclothes, the order for immediate march was countermanded; still we were to hold ourselves ready to move at a moment's warning. The authorities knew not what to do, and were distracted in their councils; by the arrival of one express after another, bringing intelligence of the "Prescott invasion" and various others, only known by report.

Rumors of an intended assault upon their own town, induced them to get rid of us at all hazards. A retrograde movement was not practicable; it was therefore determined to go on to Quebec, and run the gauntlet with the "rebels of Lower Canada." But the greatest difficulty now presented was, the procuring an adequate guard to accompany us, the fear of the Patriot forces ran so high. However, about ten A.M. the escort was ready, and we again embarked. Our boat, this time, was the "Neptune," Capt. Bullock, who received us on the bow, where we stood, or sat, on the bare deck, for the whole day, in a drizzling rain—being refused permission to go under the promenade, where was unoccupied space sufficient to accommodate a hundred or more persons. We touched for a moment at Lancaster, where the excitement prevailed in as great a degree as at Cornwall; and as the dusky clouds of evening were falling about us, we approached the low, muddy looking Coto Du Lac, just within the precints of Lower Canada, and the spot where Mrs. Wait so providentially met Sir George, on her return from Quebec. As we touched the wharf, lawyer McDonald, of St. Catharines, stepped on board; and after inquiring of my family, and my probable destiny, told me of the defeat of the habitans, with immense slaughter—the sacking and burning of their villages—the destruction of families and property; and ended with saying, "that's the way! To destroy the crows, you must burn their nests, and exterminate their young." Inhuman idea, thought I; yet it might be well if it had not been suggested to other minds than his; for the highest men, in this portion of the British realm, possessed the same barbarous opinion, and acted upon it to the fullest extent. This policy was simply but forcibly illustrated by a poor fellow, the pilot of the boat, who said, with tears on his cheeks, in his broken English, "de poor woman and de childs ran in de woods from the soldiers, and by'm by they come back—no house, no home, no pork, no bread! What can dey do? Lie down in de snow freeze starve, die! Oh mon Dieu!"

From the village we were taken in French "tumbrils," to the old fort, some distance below. Two pairs (four men) were placed in each cart, and drawn by one horse. The roads were so muddy and bad, that it was often necessary for us to get down, and extricate the empty cart from the ruts. Still the inhuman guard thought proper to add his weight to the already too heavy load, which was sure to create tumultuous altercations between them and the drivers. The darkness was so extreme that it became necessary to come to a halt, until lanterns could be procured, by the light of which we succeeded in arriving at the *old mud* fortress about eight at night, completely covered with mud; and were shown into one of the guard rooms, so small that we could not all lie or sit down at the same time; necessarily we were forced to lie upon the floor by turns, in our wet and muddy clothes, and with all our irons on. Every effort to procure food for the night was unavailing; so recourse was again had to the bag, which, with a small crust of bread, preserved from breakfast, supplied us for supper. Our management on this occasion, was rather laughable, and I cannot omit relating it: when we had concluded upon making tea, a difficulty presented itself, as to how we should obtain hot water; but that was happily obviated, by a lucky thought of one of the number, who produced a small tin basin, in which the water was boiled, and tea made for two persons, who drank it, and retired to their couch, upon "the soft side of a plank," to make room for two others; and so on, in rotation, until toward the "end of the row," when the first retiring had to get up and give place to the last; thus occupying nearly the whole night in taking *tea*; and happy were we, too, that so much comfort was left to us. However, the next day we made up for our night of fasting. The guards were the Glengary militia whose duty it was to maintain possession of the fort. Their wives, daughters, and sweethearts, made them a visit, bringing fruits, vegetables, and other comforts, *rarities in warrior's messes*, who sympathised in our misfortunes, and taught their friends to do so too, sharing their provisions with us, and making our situation more endurable. They were all Highlanders, and recognized in McLeod, a "genuine McLude of Skie," by his manly bearing, form, and make, which, in fact, would have done honor to the "kilts and tartans."

The aspect of affairs below, rendered our immediate progress imprudent, and we were, therefore, detained for the day.

Parker and myself were permitted to walk in the parade ground, with an armed man at our back. We passed several respectable looking Frenchmen, who saluted us with evident emotion, taking off their hats, and gazing at us with intense anxiety, and countenances distorted with agony. I "marked the Gael," as he walked by us, and saw the tear of sympathy glisten in his eye, as our chains rattled along upon the frozen ground. I accosted him, and said, "my good fellow, you manifest a commiseration for the miseries of your fellow men, who wear the chains of our unhappy government." He understood and spoke English very well; and replied, in accents of wo, "Canada, unhappy, poor, torn to pieces, *burnt up*, by that bad tyrant,

Gen. Colborne. We are very good reformers, but must turn out, or be burnt up too, like our poor neighbors, the Frenchmen." Then shaking his head, forbodingly turned away, and would say no more, notwithstanding our repeated attempts to draw him out. Toward evening, we were visited by Mr. Adams, commissariat of the station, through whose influence we were relieved of the cuffs, for the following night, and a part of our number taken to another room.

The morning of the 15th opened with a heavy wind up the river, rendering futile an attempt to proceed by water, in a derham boat, down the rapids, that intervenes between this and the village of the Cascades; consequently it was necessary to return, and pass down by land. The two passenger wagons used there, in that season of year, and several tumbrils, were pressed, into which we got and were driven off. The roads were shocking bad, and we could not go beyond a walk. We had scarcely started, before a terrible storm of rain, snow and sleet, came up, driving into our faces with unremitting violence for several hours. It completely covered us with one sheet of ice, from head to foot, giving us more the appearance of icy statues than living beings; and I am sure some of the less warmly clad felt so too. Just as we were entering the precints of the Cedars, a small village about half way from the Coto to the Cascades, where we halted for a half hour, the 71st regiment of regulars, on their way to the Upper Province, met us, fresh from the scenes of conflagration, carnage, and ruin. Thousands of the volunteers, men from the dregs of society; and the militia, loaded with the booty and plunder of Beauharnois followed in their wake. This scum of society, this offscouring of the Canadas, or, I might say, of the world, exhibited an inconceivably disgusting appearance. They went along, without the least order or discipline, in one confused, tumultuous mass; cursing, swearing, singing, and loudly exulting in the destruction and misery they had caused. They had pressed hundreds of French horses and carts, to transport their plunder; and poor, dumb animals! they suffered severely the brutal passions of those hands of legal robbers— those enemies to order, law and right; we passed several of these horses overthrown in the mud, and undergoing an inhuman castigation, ineffectual in making them rise. In some instances, the poor habitan willingly received the blows designed for his prostrate horse. This mass of human beings filled the road for miles, and I should imagine they numbered three or four thousand; and in their rear, as if to drive them onward, came our old *friend*, Major Arthur, with his staff, and a company of regulars. He rode up to the wagons, and demanded what prisoners they had? On being informed, he ordered a halt; and the prisoners to get down and proceed on foot, while he was determined to occupy the teams for his own especial use. This arbitrary desire created a deal of altercation; but our noble spirited Highlanders, were faithful to their charge; and although the gallant Major, in the heat of the dispute, dismounted in rage, breathing threats against our guards they maintained our right to the teams, well knowing it was an utter impossibility for us to walk *several* miles, with chains dragging to catch every protuberance on the road.

It was in utter darkness that we arrived at the Cascades a distance of fourteen miles from the Coto. Here we were obliged to remain near an hour in the wagons before a shelter could be obtained for us. Finally, a room just vacated by a party of volunteer guards, was procured. They, providentially for us, left a kettle of boiled potatoes in one corner of the fire place, which were eaten without other sauce than hunger, and only supplied about two to a man—a small supper, indeed, for men who had spent a whole day in a terrible storm, without food. The rain and sleet had congealed upon our external garments, not penetrating at all; we were, therefore, comparatively comfortable, when we threw our weary bodies upon the floor, and endeavored to betake ourselves to sleep, as well as circumstances would permit.

The storm raged with terrible fury for nearly the whole night, as if all the elements were combined to render nature frightful. It was long after I lay down 'ere I could compose myself to sleep; not but that I needed rest and repose, yet it was driven from me by the amount of horrors I had witnessed that day. My mind conjured up scenes of wretchedness and death, by exposure to the pitiless storm, of thousands of poor houseless Patriots, who, with their wives and children, had been, within the last three days, driven to seek a hiding place in the woods, from the persecutions of their fiend-like pursuers. I saw them vainly endeavoring to find shelter from the blast by skulking beneath the trunks of trees and the leafless boughs of the forest oak, without food, without clothing, and daring not, under the fear of death, to return to the spot where their homes *had* been, but *now* were *not*. Oh, I felt as if each new burst of the tempest carried grim death to some helpless victim, and every fresh gust of the roaring wind sounded a funeral knell for some unhappy soul, severed from its clay tenement by the hand of barbarity! Oh, how sad were their sufferings as pictured to my mind! yet might not those very persons who were then shrieking in the last struggles of nature, be in a more enviable situation than I, who was condemned to not only share every vicissitude of bodily sufferance but undergo every infamy, disgrace, debasement, and mental distress, that could be heaped upon man. Yet I saw myself borne up through all I had yet experienced with unanticipated fortitude. However, had all things been opened at once to my view, and all the *evils* I had felt been poured down on my devoted head at once, despair, or at least, despondency would have been my lot. Even then I knew not the amount I had yet to endure, and well for me that the dim uncertain future was shaded by the curtain of merciful silence, so that when it was withdrawn, and slowly as I could bear, came sorrow and severe anguish, the spirit was enabled to abide all, for it knew not the worst.

At a late hour my melancholy musings gave way to the sacred balm of religion, which calmed my heart's turbulent passions, and checked its transports of grief. I heartily commended my sleeping companions, with all suffering humanity, to the care of kind heaven, and throwing myself unreservedly upon its proffered protection, sunk into a placid repose. But repose could not last, the clanking of my companions' chains, and the pains arising from my own, aroused me at a very early hour to recollection and misery. While awaiting the passage boat, we observed several flat-bottomed boats approaching from the opposite shore, where the greatest destruction had taken place, loaded with cattle, produce, and household goods of every description, though the wind blew still quite fresh.

About 12, the steamer Dragon arrived from Beauharnois, also freighted with every sort of plunder, as well as a number of militia, part of the army we met the day previous, who had remained behind to glut the spirit of destruction by an extra act of conflagration and ruin. By this boat we received a supply of provisions, which, you may well suppose, we greatly needed, having fasted for the last thirty hours.

As soon as the Dragon had discharged her ill-gotten cargo, we were transferred to her. She lay at the point made by the confluence of the Grand Ottawa and the St. Lawrence, two of the noblest rivers of British America. They afford, for various divisions of this vast country, great natural facilities for commerce and manufactures. The scene was a grand one, and gave rise to speculations on the probable greatness of the Canadas, at some future day, when they would have effectually "arisen in their might," and shaken off the tyrant's yoke, and paralysed the hand of oppression. I never did, nor do I now, doubt the ultimate consummation of such an event.

The boat soon put off, and left far behind these prospects predictive of ultimate greatness, and Canada's elevation soon gave place to pictures of a vividly opposite caste. I remained on deck with my yoke fellow, (for the day was tolerably serene,) to witness the noble, the beautiful scenery, on the banks of the grand St. Lawrence.

A shudder, a feeling akin to horror shot through my frame, as my eyes were first directed to the yet smoking ruins of a proscribed Canadian's homestead. Every building that might have afforded the slightest shelter to man or beast, was burnt to the ground. Every tree cut down, and every particle of food destroyed or carried away. We soon swept past this mark of a tyrant's displeasure, to the view of another scene still more heart rending; it appeared to have been the residence of a person of considerable wealth, for numerous piles of smoking embers were observed, which, from appearances, betokened the building to have been of no slight magnitude. Though all had now vanished but the ashes, and the poor forlorn destitute beings who had once made their roofs echo with the sounds of gladness, perhaps of sacred worship, had just ventured from their hiding place, and were apparently hunting about the premises if perchance the remorseless incendiaries had left undestroyed one morsel whereby a raging hunger might be appeased. There stood a mother and five children, vainly weeping over the ruins of their home, as if their tears could restore what they had lost; no doubt a husband, parent, brother, or friend were weltering in their own blood, or if living, groaning in irons, reserved in dungeons, as victims for the insatiable gallows, or exiled from their families, whose sufferings they could not know the extent of, and distracted in the knowledge that Sir John Colborne was relentless in his furious revenge.

Oh, how many of these brave, honest and virtuous Canadians have suffered in themselves and families, all of the refined cruelty, insult, indignity and aggression that the mind of an Aylmar, a Gosford with his colleagues, and a Colborne, with his merciless horde of freebooting ravishers, could invent. And for what? Because they entertained laudable desires of exercising their restricted prerogatives in curbing, as far as was in their power, the avarice, and licentiousness of the arbitrary governors. Because they, in youth's bright visions, beheld what was due to humanity, and longed to enjoy the fruits of their own industry, in peace and in liberty. Because they had looked across the narrow waters, and envied the happy freedom of their neighbors, where each could eat his own bread, beneath his own roof, amid his happy family, in joy and content. Where he could look about him and say, "these are mine, and none can dispossess me; I can enjoy my own, undisturbed by intestine commotion, murderous factions, or an avaricious despot's glance."

Amid these sad meditations, as if to heighten the melancholy, a cry of "look yonder!" directed my attention to the opposite shore, (eight or ten miles distant,) where the work of destruction was beginning anew. The flames were just bursting from several houses and barns, hitherto unscathed. At that moment, the steward of the boat came up to where we were, and I enquired of him why such devastation was still continuing when the insurrection was supposed to be wholly quelled. He replied that a "company of the blood-hounds of Colborne were going the rounds with his orders, to visit every hamlet and farmstead, and whenever the male proprietor could not be found, to burn and destroy his possessions without remorse." Horrid barbarity! cruel order! by which thousands of hapless victims were rendered roofless and foodless in the commencement of a North American winter.

We touched at Beauharnois, a small village, formerly containing several hundred houses, but now only filled with smouldering ruins, exhibiting the traces of the demon of destruction. Here, but the day before, under the eye of Colborne, every excess had been perpetrated; houses reduced to ashes; property of every description , and furniture were broken up and strewed the streets. Women of every grade, age, or condition, insulted, violated, murdered. Col. McDonald, of the Glengary militia, and sherriff of Kingston, writes as follows regarding the destruction of this village: "We proceeded towards Beauharnois by a forced march, burning and laying waste the country as we went along, and it was a most distressing and heart-rending scene, to see this fine settlement completely destroyed, and the houses burned and laid in ashes; and I understand the whole country around St. Charles experienced the same. The wailing of the women and children, in beholding their houses in flames and property destroyed, their husbands, brothers, fathers and sons dragged along prisoners, and such of them as did not appear were supposed to be at the rebel camp." In the destruction of this and other places, the orange faction were the most prominent actors. And from this same compact of state and orangeism have sprung two thirds of the woes that the distracted Canadas have endured. All other scenes of modern warfare, even among the barbarous nations of the east and south, were faint pictures of cruelty when compared to the atrocities in Lower Canada, in 1838. The heroes of St. Dennis, St. Charles, St. Eustache, Beauharnois, and many other places, can boast of "heroic deeds" unparalleled in the annals of modern history, for their warfare was carried on principally against defenceless women and children. They will walk forth in this world with the mark of villains and murderers on their foreheads, and go down to the grave unhonored and unwept! while their conduct brands the government they serve with ignominy and deserved contumely.

The officers of our boat entered pretty deeply into the chance of speculation, offered by the scattered property of the murdered and exiled families of this ill-fated town. The deck was piled with goods and household furniture, of rare and rich qualities, and several horses, that had been brought to the wharf and sold there for one dollar per head, were carried, on board, to Lachine.

I saw a few of the French, who had been left, for some cause or another. They appeared extremely dejected, and forlorn. Oh! what bitter pangs I experienced at the sight; and glad was I to have the order given for departure. I prevailed on Parker to go below, (for the bow cabin, or "steerage," was allotted to us,) where I endeavored to shut out the thought of what I had witnessed within the last two hours, and drown my sadness in the oblivion of sleep. But in this, "I had reckoned without my host;" for the atmosphere was humid and cold—such as was calculated to totally repel sleep or rest. At first, I was at a loss to account for it, and the fetid smell of the cabin; but was soon informed, that this was the boat that had been taken, a few days previous, at Beauharnois, by the French Patriots, when it was scuttled and sunk; and but two days since, raised and repaired.

The oppressiveness of the air soon drove us to the deck again, when I, to my no small gratification, discovered that we had passed the "proscribed districts." I was highly delighted with the fine scenery on the banks of this wonderful thoroughfare. It was not such as would strike the romantic beholder with awe, or with wonder; but its apparent unobtrusiveness, with occasional glimpses of distant mountains, and adjacent forests, were well calculated to excite, in the mind, a pleasing sensation of delight—a sort of buoyant gladness, stimulated by the appearance of the landscape, and the neatness of the small French cottages, contrasted with the magnificant river, on whose pellucid bosom our boat floated like a thing animate. These fine, comfortable looking fields and farms, hardly assorted with the ruined estates we had just passed. The demon of destruction had not visited here.

As near as could be judged, in such a bleak season, the fields and whole country, was in an unique state of culture, and the appearance would have been congenial to an enthusiastic admirer of a grand uniformity of natural and artificial scenery united. But I must again bid you adieu, and defer, for my next, a continuation of our passage toward Quebec.

I remain, dear sir,
Yours, &c. &c.

6

MONTREAL TO QUEBEC

Ashgrove, near Oatlands, V.D.L.
September, 1840.

To — —,
My Dear Sir: —
Our next landing was at Lachine, a small village, nine miles from Montreal;
between which places the navigation of the river is impeded, by a succession of small falls or rapids; around which there is a canal cut, only navi-
gated by small batteaux, drawn by horses. We disembarked about sunset,
amid a large concourse of people, who supposed us to be of the prisoners
taken at Beauharnois, and consequently loaded us with insult and scoffs.
We paid but little attention to these noisy burlesques of the human race;
and I felt as I remarked to the civil officers who walked by us, that such *grat-
ulations* were the most honorable we could receive from men who were evidently a part of the sackers of Beauharnois, and the murderers of men,
women, and children. With the setting of the sun, the clouds arose, and a
terrible storm of rain and wind commenced, that continued to rage for
some hours, then settled down into a cold snow storm. The batteau into
which we got was open, and towed by one horse, and managed by two
Frenchmen and a boy. The men were driven about like dogs; and dare not
murmur, for there was no redress. Several clumsy, inefficient looking
locks intervene on this short canal; at each of which, stoppages and delays
were inevitable. At about nine P.M. we arrived at Montreal, and ran into
one of the basins, where we lay exposed to the snow and cold for some
hours, awaiting the reappearance of one of the civil officers, who had
gone on from Lachine, to procure lodging for us. But he did not make his
appearance, having found some friend, whose cup proved too potent for
his weak head to admit of his moving abroad that night, much to our discomfort. After waiting for some hours, the remaining civil officer determined on moving around to the garrison, and landing on the beach; which
was not effected without much danger and difficulty. He then left us

standing there, in the storm, and went away to find a lodging. He did not return for more than an hour, when he took us into a small guard room, in the middle of the city, leaving the baggage upon the shore, subject to the storm, and to plunder; the latter of which was only prevented by the darkness. When we were introduced to our room, the great town clock was striking twelve; and in about two hours, our baggage followed. The space allotted to us, was what had formerly been the inner room of a lawyer's office, eight by sixteen feet, with a "military deal bed," calculated for eight persons to sleep on. In this small hole, it was impossible to sit down, as it was scarce practicable to stand. We were all horror-stricken at the prospect of spending the night in such an unhappy situation—some sunk to the floor, wearied under a load of frozen clothes and care. I have oftened wondered how it could possibly happen, that we did not all despair at once, and settle down in a fatal despondency; but even in that suffocating situation, the jest went round, and the affected laugh sounded with a vain effort "to drive dull care away." I thought of Virgil's picture of a cell in the infernal region, and laughed at the idea fancy had conjured up, while I longed for a light to realize it. A light at last came, and showed imagination's sketch no exaggeration.

The light was in the hand of the Town Major, who was forcibly struck with the scene; for an exclamation of extreme surprise broke from him the moment the door opened and he beheld twenty-three men, chained and hand cuffed, pent up in a room where twelve would find it difficult to lie down. Some were lying stretched upon the cold floor, sinking through sheer exhaustion, and the closeness of the place we were in. Others were standing over them, leaning against the wall, happy in such support. Some were loudly calling for water, which could not be supplied, as the guard had but little in, and could not leave the station to go for more.

The sight of the Town Major's sympathising face, and the civilities offered by the few gentlemen who accompanied, relieved us of much of the despondency that was clouding our hearts. He left us with an assurance, that water would be immediately supplied, and other lodgings provided, for at least a part of the number. A pail of water came, and was handed in; but, alas, no cup! no, not a tin canteen could be found to drink out of. I will leave you to imagine what course we pursued in regard to what every man among us was almost dying for, and which was actually larger than we could find space for. The pail, nevertheless, was soon emptied, and afforded a seat or footstool for some one. After remaining in this crowded and fainting state for two hours or more, we were partially relieved, by the removal of eight to other quarters. Nothing was supplied for food, and all we could raise, was a small quantity of bread and meat, I had providentially saved from our meal, on the steamboat. We partook of that morsel with a devotional gratitude to God, who giveth all things; then commended ourselves to His care, sought sleep on the bare floor.

For my part, I fell at once into a deep slumber, and dreamed of home's happy fireside; heard the guileless laugh, and felt the playful, *stolen* kiss of affection. Often, since my feet have been debarred "tracing the woods, the lawns, the flowery meads;" and my eyes have viewed aught but misery, and wo, and wretchedness; and my heart from feeling any thing but a loneliness, hopelessness, anguish, and deep insult, I have felt happy, aye, vividly happy, in a review of the bright and joyous visions of midnight. Yes! though my head lay upon the hard floor, and all my bones were aching with the pains of wearied out nature, and all comfort forbidden, yet a kind, overruling Providence has so ordered it, that no despot, however powerful, can chain the independent mind. In the forgetfulness of sleep, it will revert to the joyous scenes of former days, that leave upon its tablets, blissful sensations to engage the waking hours, and draw it forcibly from corroding thoughts.

I must not omit to mention a circumstance that occurred here, though trifling, as it had a great weight in bringing about a subsequent occurrence, that operated much to my discomfort. During the night, before any had been removed, Vernon and Gemmel, who were coupled together, determined on procuring more ease and liberty, broke the lock that fastened their cuffs, and began to saw the chain, when they were interrupted by the Town Major's entrance. They were, after going on board the steamer for Quebec, punished for it, by being forced to wear another pair, for some hours, after the remainder had been relieved.

The next morning brought the civil officers, whose flinty natures, all our sufferings from wet clothes, and swollen arms, could not move to a single act of pity. We vainly entreated a removal of the "wrist bands," only long enough to admit of our throwing off our upper garments. They departed without even administering one comfortable word, or one morsel of bread to the calls of hunger. At noon, came a few of the officers of the twenty-fourth regiment, who, after remarking that we were "fine looking fellows, and would well befit the British uniform," enquired whether we had any "complaints to make." We exhibited our wrists, but with that they could not interfere: we then told of our long fast and thirst, which could not be remedied, unless they thought proper to order otherwise. They replied, that Governor Colborne was there, and we would, most probably be delivered up to his charge consequently, until the delivery was made, and arrangements completed, we must remain in "statu quo." However they promised a meal from their own mess, in the absence of other provisions; yet it was three P.M. before it came. While we were devouring it, the order for our removal, forthwith, to the steamboat, arrived; and we were directed to pocket our uneaten provisions. The men who had been separated from us for the night, rejoined us. They had been taken to the garrison, where the soldiers shared their messes and beds with them.

A numerous guard received us at the door, where a vast concourse was rapidly collecting, to "look at the Upper Canadians," Followed by them, we were marched down Notre Dame street to the wharf, and embarked on board the "British North America," bound for Quebec. A variety of feelings seemed to actuate the multitude; for some expressed a sympathy, while others mocked; some pitied, while others derided; and many employed us to maintain a "good courage, as it was a glorious cause we were suffering in." We were placed in the bow cabin, where was burning, in a large stove, a roaring fire. This was exhilarating to us, who had long been without so great a *luxury*. Through the kind influence of some gentlemen passengers, and the Captain, we were released from the torturing manacles, and enjoyed a respite from pain; an alleviation that weary nature profited by. At an early hour we turned into our bedless berths; and for the first time, since leaving Fort Henry, passed a night of uninterrupted repose. We awoke in the morning, greatly refreshed and invigorated, though with a strong appetite for a sound meal, that did not remain long unappeased.

Immediately after partaking our breakfast we hurried to the deck, and hailed the bright sun with uncommon cheerfulness.

The ride down this part of the St. Lawrence, was a glorious and a pleasant one, and I enjoyed the prospects with unsurpassed delight. About noon the heights bounding the plains of Abraham were visible, up whose rocky shelves the bold and adventurous Wolf wended his way to glory and to death; and where the valorous and gallant Montcalm, poured out the red streams of life, in defence of the chivalry of France.

Every word I have read of this celebrated spot, animatingly recurred to my memory; and my bosom burned to view, more closely, the landscape of those plains, richer in soul-stirring incident to me, than would be the classic ground of Italy. I could have gazed, for hours, with veneration, upon the monument that bears, jointly, the names of those two heroes; and which not only perpetuates their memory, but also impressions of the former power, chivalry, and contests of two great nations. The magnanimity, on the part of one, however, I felt by a glance at my chains, was dwindled down to a low, revengeful despotism; and as a counterpoise to this lasting monument of *discolored* fame, pillars that would hereafter be erected to the memory of the self-devoted Lount, Mathews, Morrow, and many others, would stand as still more enduring monuments of her shame.

The ice had delayed us so much, that, instead of arriving at the usual hour of six in the morning, it was one P.M. when we approached the wharf. Our presence attracted a vast multitude, who betrayed the same varied feelings we had seen exhibited at Toronto and Montreal. But here let me say, to the honor of the habitans, that I did not witness a single gibe or insult proceed from any wearing the garb of the French; but, on the contrary, I observed, in all their countenances, that mute, expressive sympathy, which always cheers the wounded hearts of men wearing the chains of unjust oppression. I even heard them stoutly upbraid those who had raised their voices in unmerited derision; and I doubly esteemed them for their devotional Patriotism and sympathy.

No disposition to get up more than a hiss was apparent until we had just emerged within the gate, when a ragged, contemptible wretch, with an

Irish accent and an orange badge, came up to Parker and myself, who were walking in the rear, and swore we "were just the men to take the place of his renegade countryman, Theller, and the d—d Yankee sympathizer, Dodge," who, it appears, had made a remarkable escape from the "impregnable citadel." The name was caught up by a hundred voices, and echoed, with various epithets of contempt and applause. One individual near me, wished in his heart we "might make as good an exit from the walls of Quebec as they did, God bless them!" The streets were narrow, and so thronged with people curious to see us, that it was a difficult matter for the regulars to force a passage through; while it was with the utmost toil and pain that we dragged our chained limbs up the icy streets, that enter the city with considerable acclivity. I looked at the frowning towers and the well mounted batteries as we passed, and admired the strength as well as the care manifested to guard this ancient city from the attacks of its enemies. I had but little chance for observation, but what I did see of the buildings, gave me no favorable impression of its wealth or cleanliness; and from the compressed state in which the houses stand, and the narrowness of the streets one would suppose the city lacked room for its inhabitants.

At length, after a weary march of an hour, we "fetched up" at the door of the old City Jail, where Mr. Jeffries, the keeper, met and led us to a large room in the north wing, with a row of dismal looking cells on either side. I had supposed that Cape Diamond was the place destined for our reception, but was soon undeceived by the muster and delivery of our *noble selves* to the Sheriff of Quebec, who proceeded, to divest our wrists of the cuffs, which had been put on again on landing, after a respite from Montreal.

A cup of tea and a piece of coarse bread was offered us for supper. Several gentlemen came in during the evening to see and converse with us—particularly a couple of editors, tories of course, as all independent and liberal papers have been suppressed, while "their editors were locked up." Before retiring, or rather, at eight, the jailor came in, accompanied by two turnkeys, one bearing two or three large bunches of keys, and the other a large hammer. The hammer was to us a welcome sight, for we supposed it was for the purpose of knocking off our chains; but in this we were mistaken, as the bearer forthwith proceeded to sound every iron bar constituting the guard to the windows, a precautionary step counselled by the then late fortunate escape through the grated windows of the citadel. Armed guards were doubled about the prison, and one walked continually under each cell window, occasionally raising himself up and peering in, lest we might be engaged in something *wrong*. Our bedding here became very useful, as that supplied was too scanty for the cold weather.

The next morning, a large pot of oatmeal gruel, with a quart of molasses, and a half pound of bread, was brought for our breakfast. The gruel but few of our number could partake of, having never before seen such "stuff" substituted for provision. It was soon changed for something more palatable at the instance of some unknown friends, who generously offered to foot the difference. The sheriff kindly acceded to our repeated desire, and freed us from the iron incumbrances which we had worn without intermission for ten days. At the same time, he intimated, as a *probable* event, a removal to England, provided a passage could be obtained for us, yet that, on account of the lateness of the season, was very doubtful. I wrote by return of the Kingston Deputy, to Mrs. Wait, informing her that I had no doubt she would next hear from me in England. Each person prepared his letters of farewell, and then commenced a general ablution of person and clothing, preparatory to further measures; knowing that if we were sent on, it would be prematurely. While incarcerated in Quebec, the nine persons who had availed themselves of the privilege granted by an "ex post facto" law, and petitioned for transportation instead of standing the "fearful trial," served upon the sheriff a protest against the sentence being carried into full effect, and employed an attorney to attend to the affair for them. It proved of no avail. Those of us who had undergone a trial in Niagara, deemed it more politic to rest our cases for the present, and immediately on arrival in England, throw ourselves upon the justice and good feeling of that government, rather than make the slightest appeal to the equity of a man whose fraudulent and dishonest measures had conduced much to produce the rebellion in Upper Canada, and whose arbitrary proceedings during a three months administration had filled Lower Canada with blood and murder, with conflagration and ruin.

For my own part, I had not the slightest idea of going farther than England, and would prefer crossing thither to remaining subject to the Provincial authorities for the winter, therefore hailed the news with eager delight, when, on the 20th Nov., the sheriff (Mr. Sewell) informed us that our passage was engaged, and the only necessary delay was to give time for fitting up a "cabin" to stow us away in. I wrote again to U.C., without the least uneasiness, confident of returning free within a year at least, particularly if I was held there until Mrs. Wait should arrive, whom I felt assured of meeting there in the spring. But the sequel will show how sadly misplaced was my confidence in their justice and clemency.

Providentially, we had a little money remaining, with which we laid in what necessary sea stores was deemed most indispensable. The prisoners could not all command means to supply what was actually necessary, and none but Mr. Parker, had more than sufficient for a very small stock. Our removal from Fort Henry having been so sudden, that no time was given to communicate our necessities to our friends, who could have provided what we wanted. I remembered the kind sympathy shown by the Lord Bishop Mountaine to Mrs. Wait, on a former occasion, and wrote him expressive of my gratitude. He was absent from his residence, but his chaplain, Rev. George Makie, came to see me, and brought a number of Testaments, Prayer Books, and other religious volumes, which he begged I would distribute among my companions. I gratefully accepted his kindness, and have brought many of them with me to this country, where publications of every kind are very scarce and dear; and I hope they will be serviceable in moralizing the wretched inhabitants, for I can assure you there is indeed much necessity for it. Some of our number were also destitute of proper clothing, and an appeal was therefore made, but vainly, to the authorities; yet successfully to individual sympathy. The supply was all that was actually necessary to shield them from the cold, but no regard was had to appearance. On the 22d, the sheriff informed us that we might prepare, as that day we should embark. He hoped we would find our passage an agreeable one, but was fearful we would suffer unnecessary restraint, "as Captain Morton is greatly terrified, for he imagines you to be a parcel of *dare-devils*, capable of undertaking anything, and I fear that will be a cause of not a little inconvenience to you." So said Sewell, and such we found was the truth. In answer to a question, he said, "the quarters designed for your accommodation have been examined by a board of magistrates, (or directors) who pronounced them proper and comfortable, and so they ought to be too, for the owner gets 25 pounds per head for taking you 'home', and furnishing you with provisions." He also informed us that "a number of French felons, of the worst class, whose crimes were theft, burglary, and highway robbery, were to go in the same ship. You will, of course, for your own credit, have no communication with them, as they are bound together by the various ties of evil and corrupt associations, while they would feel no scruple in stealing the last morsel you had to eat. They have been addicted to every vice under heaven from infancy, and with some of them this is the third sentence." Such was the sheriff's picture of beings the Governor, Sir John Colborne, had selected as companions for us to England, for the purpose, no doubt, of throwing upon our characters appearances of deeper stigma.

The city was filled with rumors regarding the unprecedented escape of Theller and Dodge, from the hitherto impregnable fort. "But Yankees are the *devils* for liberty, and iron grates, stone walls, or bayonets can not detain them from it." They have achieved a wonderful deed; they desired freedom, they strove for it, and they gained it; and may they enjoy it for ever! We were informed "the authorities were well convinced the plan never could have prospered but through prompt aid from without." Suspicion had rested upon the guard, but that was allayed by the fact of the sentinel being so thoroughly drugged; and "hundred-eyed fame" implicated many a man, whose assistance could have been rendered in no other way than through good wishes and prayers, yet who would, had an opportunity offered, have periled their lives in accomplishing what was happily effected without them.

We saw by papers, stealthily obtained, that these two men had been received in New York at the same time with Messrs. W. Nelson, Bouchette, Desriviers, Gauvire, Marchasault Goddeau, and Viger, from Bermuda, whither they had been arbitrarily sent by Lord Durham, and from whence they returned on account of the Governor refusing to acknowledge the authority of a Canadian Governor to control or command him. A glorious, independent principle, that resulted in the liberation of five as good men as ever trod the Canadian soil. A happy meeting indeed theirs must have

62

been, in the joy of which we heartily participated, though captives ourselves. We exulted in their freedom, and looked confidently forward to the time when our own lot would be as happy.

We read with dejected hearts the total failure of the numerous irruptions along the whole frontier of the two Canadas, and were intensely distressed and excited by the unhappy fate of many of our personal acquaintances, who fell in the field, or were butchered in cold blood by the notorious Prince. Yet I did not mourn those who fell gallantly fighting, so much as I did the poor captives, whose fate (Judging from what would have been mine had there been no restraint exercised over Sir George Arthur) would be a thousand times worse. "They must expiate their crimes (love of freedom) on the bloody gallows." Those in the Upper Province were in the hands of "a fiend whose delight was blood," and who, for his atrocities in Van Dieman's Land, had deservedly received the cognomen of "Arthur, the Bloody Executioner." May God deliver them from his hands, and disappoint his dark revenge, was the sincere prayer of my heart when I had finished the tale of wo.

At about eleven, came the blacksmith with his hammer and anvil, accompanied by a man bearing our chains, with the sound of which we had become so familiar, that it failed to create much sensation now. We were prepared by having all our things packed away, and our clothes on to shield us from the severe cold. The chains were riveted on our legs as before, but unfortunately for Mr. Parker and myself, the one worn and notched by Messrs. Gemmel and Vernon, as before related, fell to us. These chains and a company of regulars were not sufficient security in passing through a walled town, but the execrable cuffs must be added to our equipments, perhaps for our comfort or a peculiar indignity. Yes, it must be so! for I have never known the British government, or any of its emissaries omit these, though there was no necessity for them. We were driven from the door on a number of sleds to the dock, where a vast multitude was collected, among whom I could not perceive the slightest inclination to rudeness, but the tear of sympathy glistened in many an eye, and if I could judge by appearances, many a heartfelt prayer went up for our welfare.

The ship in which we were to embark rode two miles from shore. As we seated ourselves in the yawl, where eleven felons were before us, one universal acclaim rent the air, "for our safe and speedy return to our homes." When we shoved off, I could not refrain repeating Moore's beautiful and pathetic farewell to Erin. The French in the boat sung a plaintive French ditty, that was responded to by those on shore, with such a deep pathos that the man must have possessed a heart of adamant who could have listened without tearful emotions.

But I must make the embarkation and passage the subject of another letter.

I remain, dear sir,
Yours, &c. &c.

7

QUEBEC TO LIVERPOOL

Ashgrove, near Oatlands, V.D.L.
November, 1840.

To ——,

My Dear Sir: —

The close of November is very inclement in Lower Canada; and you may, therefore, be well assured, that we anticipated no pleasure in the voyage to England but could not possibly have dreamed of the slightest approach to the horrors we were about to be subjected to, on board the Capt. Ross, a barque lying with anchor hove apeak, awaiting our arrival. She was owned by two brothers, Messrs. Frost's one of whom resided in Liverpool, and the other at Quebec. The latter accompanied us from the dock, and informed us that the "cabin," prepared for our reception, was fit for the Governor's use; and Capt. Morton had his instructions to treat us with forbearance and furnish us good provisions; and, said he, "you will find yourselves uselessly encumbered with your sea stores;" and that Capt. M. was a good, kind man, who would act a generous part towards us, to whom he would introduce Mr. Parker and myself.

As soon as our yawl struck the ship, the anchor was tripped, the sails shook out, and the ship got under way.

We found some difficulty and danger in climbing up the ship's side, but were assisted by the board of Magistrates, who, with Mr. Hunter, (son-in-law, to the jailer, Mr. Jeffries,) were there before us. A hurried delivery was made of the prisoners, by the Sheriff to "Capt. Digby Morton," when all left but Mr. Frost and Hunter. We were taken directly aft, where the master stood in evident tremor, which I supposed the effect of the cold, though I thought of what the Sheriff had said.

The day was uncommonly severe, and it was with no small pleasure Mr. P. and myself, who stood first, found ourselves *searched,* and turned below. But ah! what was our horror and dismay when we discovered the wretched appearance of the place we were to occupy. We called immediately to Mr. Hunter, whom we desired to look about it, and give his opinion. He did so, and said, "it was more like being calculated for beasts, than for human beings to inhabit. I will go directly on shore, and make affidavit to that effect; and, if possible, get the ship detained." He did go directly away; but his endeavors were vain, if, indeed, he intended to do any thing; for the ship was under sail, and a fair wind soon drove us onward beyond the reach of his promised humanity.

When the whole number, including twenty-three state prisoners, and eleven felons, had been searched, and sent below together; and the trap, or hatch of iron grates, locked down upon us, a scene of confusion and tumult commenced, which beggars description. I will not attempt it, but will only say, that P. and myself, being the first below selected what we deemed the most convenient berth, and climbed quietly into it, to give room for others; for not one half could have stood up, at the same time, in the space allotted us. The shouts and curses of the felons, fighting for preeminence, mingled with the clanking of chains, aided by the frigid chillness of the atmosphere, and the damp, fetid, smell, arising from the bilge water, created peculiar sensations of gloom, and dread, and forebodings. I gazed upon the face of every man near me, and saw that the same expression sat there that I fancied was upon my own. There was something working within the mind, that evidently bewildered and agitated it, and each dejected countenance spoke too plainly of an appalling presentiment. For my own part, I felt that the last trials of life had arrived. I looked about me, and was assured that existence must be short, when surrounded with such circumstances. Indeed, it had no charms, and no hopes, save in a future world. My heart sank, and every buoy vanished from my soul. *Then* I would have given worlds to have terminated my life upon the gallows, agreeable to my original sentence; for there I should have been no useless sacrifice in the cause of Patriotism. Then I should have been honored and mourned by friends; and my corpse, though mangled, would have been laved by the tears of sympathy, and perhaps received a christian interment. But here, unknown to the world I was about to fall a victim to a death still more inhuman and disconcerting than the halter; and one that must have been dictated by private treachery. For no man would, for a moment, after entering the place, have harbored the thought of dragging on life beyond a week. I looked upon death as inevitable, and revolved in my mind every scene that must succeed, until appalled at the idea. For the first time, I shuddered at the approach of "the monster" I had formerly unshrinkingly faced in a variety of forms.

I had heard my days numbered, and seen the gallows erected as their finisher, with scarce a wish to have it other wise; yet now, to become a victim in the manner here in view, and my body cast into the deep, a "loathed thing," unhonored, unwept, and, perhaps, my fate never known! was a thought I could not endure. There is an indefinite something so revolting in the thought of our bodies, though "lifeless lumps," being consigned to a watery grave, without christian rites, or to a stranger's tomb, without sympathy, that it adds the climax of dismay, and unmans the soul. The mind cannot long remain in this agonising intensity. It must either shake it off with a violent effort, and rise superior to every extreme, or sink at once into a lethargic dispiritedness, when the soul must pine, and mope, and weaken, and at last utterly decay, beneath its corroding influence. The buoyant heart, or active spirit, may occasionally fall into the latter state; but reason will soon emancipate it, and revive drooping hope; for, with such, "while there is life, there is hope." But there are those, unused to disappointment, easily discouraged in mind, whose spirits, when once bent down by despair, can never revert to natural buoyancy, but will drag on their tenements imperceptibly to the grave. Of these poor McLeod and McNulty, soon showed themselves a part; for they never recovered the shock their minds received at that embarkation; but gradually declined, both in bodily and mental vigor; and desponding to the last, dropped almost unconsciously into the silent tomb. I strove hard to overcome the distress of mind, and dejection of spirits, that inevitably follows such practicing upon the mysteries of the brain; and sought to bear all with becoming equanimity, and proper christian fortitude. Hope did, indeed, buoy up my soul in these trying prospects; yet it was not a hope for prolonged existence here, or reenjoying the former pleasures of this life; but a heavenly, and a purely christian hope, that operated as "an anchor to the soul," and taught me to look beyond the "vale of tears," for all I could expect of pleasure and joy. I also found a consolation in reflecting upon the intensity and purity of the faith under which I had acted, and I felt not a repentant thought, or a reflective censure, for a single act of my political career. I have frequently, since my incarceration, found, that, when insulted by malice, or oppressed by inhumanity, the heart could assume a stern fortitude, almost foreign to its nature, that arouses it to a dignified *contempt* for *fate*, while it infuses into the mind proper conceptions of our relations to Him who gave us life and being, and will not suffer "a sparrow to fall to the ground unnoticed."

Although we had undergone severe pain from cold, hunger, want of rest, taught irons, exposure to all sorts of weather, and abuse and insult, from a set of proud aristocrats, who had evidently been raised from the lowest grade, to a station above their proper sphere; yet I can safely aver, that, at our embarkation, at Quebec, commenced a series of new pains and new sufferings, far superior, in bitterness, in misery, and in producing mental anguish, than all we had before experienced; and which continued, with but little intermission, for a year.

The Capt. Ross was a small timber vessel, loaded at Montreal, with pine and oak lumber, that had, apparently, been exposed to the winter storms, and was literally covered with ice. She was the last ship bound, that season, for England, and the only hope for our conveyance. The owner was therefore applied to, and, notwithstanding her being completely filled, he concluded to charter a small portion of her for that purpose, as thirty-four persons would not be of as great weight as the lumber he would have to displace to furnish room, but they would add many hundred per cent to the freightage money. To gain which, (for he reasoned geometrically,) he would only be obliged to cut down a hole, twelve or fourteen feet square, in the mid-ships, through the frozen mass; and the boards cut out would answer all purposes for building up the berths. All the expense, therefore, would be a pound or two of nails. This *humane suggestion* was instantly acted upon; and behold, after two days, with all hands turned to, an apartment appeared, ready furnished, "that was fit for the Governor's use," and which ought for ever *to do honor to the generous originator*. When we first "went below," into that "hole of darkness," the damp, chill atmosphere, seemed to strike *through* my whole person; creating, in every joint and vein, indescribably painful sensations; and emotions of the mind, that a frigid desolation alone could produce. The blood appeared to curdle; and, trembling, shuddering, palpitating, shrunk back to the heart, and left the body cold and chill, benumbed and inanimate; obviously laboring vehemently, to regain natural perspiration—sensations that I cannot better portray than by supposing a person, when in free pulsation, plunged unprepared into bitter cold water. A considerable period elapsed before the body could return to its natural feeling. After a few days, this dreary chillness, gave way to an oppressive humidity—a suffocating warmth, caused by the air being so repeatedly inhaled; and by which, it became so vapid and putrid, that I cannot but wonder how humanity could endure it. Indeed, nothing but the especial favor of Providence, sustained us, and led us through that most trying scene.

Another thing which added much to the malignity of the atmosphere, was the fact, of none of our number being permitted to go to the upper deck, for any purpose whatever, during the first fifteen days; and consequently, there was a necessity for nuisances below, which were two common buckets, placed loosely upon the deck, beside some of the beds. The lurching of the ship often upset them. The effect this had upon the atmosphere and the cleanliness of the poor fellows who were forced to lie, (for I do not believe they could sleep,) on the deck, must be imagined, for it is too revolting to be described.

All who occupied the lower tier of berths, as well as the deck, frequently also, got the *benefit* of a sea water bath; for when the wind and waves were high, the upper deck was flooded, and the water rushed down the grated hatch, (over which only a tarpauling was loosely drawn,) until the deck was scuttled to let it off; while those occupying the upper berths were subject to the continued dripping from the lumber, of the melting ice. The bedding allowed, (beside our own,) consisted of a narrow straw mattress, and two blankets. My bed lay next the wall, and it became immediately wet, and continued so until we disembarked. A narrow shelf was occupied by poor McNulty and John Grant, one of whom could scarce maintain a place upon it; being chained together, they could not separate; therefore were obliged to lie "heads and points", or "take turns". The deck above us was pierced on each side with a hole, two by four inches, into which were settled thick "bull's eye" glasses, forming "sky lights," that only served to make darkness more visible. They did, indeed, afford light for one or two to read for a few hours in a bright day, but the book must be held immediately under the glass. One of these glasses was directly over my berth; and consequently I spent much of the time more agreeably than many others. During fifteen days I was not out of my berth for ten minutes at a time; and still I unaccountably retained my health and spirits.

A description can scarce convey the smallest idea of the real sufferings we endured; and none, but those who have experienced a storm at sea, under similar circumstances, can conceive the disorder continually raging among us. I have, since, particularly examined many places, built expressly for the condign punishment of incorrigible offenders. The "black hole" —the low, iron bound, flagged cell—the tread mill, and many other inventions for peculiar torture, in this land of fraud and infamy, (where a renowned clergyman, after being asked by George Arthur to examine and give his opinion upon a permanent gallows he had erected in view of his own piazza, said, "I have examined your new scaffold, sir, and say it will last for many years; *nine will* hang upon it *comfortably*, and eleven in one of your cases of exigency,") and positively would be understood to say, that I never witnessed one in which human beings could *not drag on* life with more comfort, and less misery, than in the hold of the barque Capt. Ross, where I spent twenty-five days; and eternal disgrace ought to follow Mr. Frost, the owner, and the members of the board of magistrates, under whose supervision he fitted it up.

The provisions were on a par with other things; and consisted of oat meal gruel for breakfast and supper. Of course, those who had any provisions themselves, eat none of that "stuff;" and for dinner, a pail of "scouse," made of "salt junk" (beef), and pieces of biscuit, boiled up together, without regard to cleanliness or relish—the meat was nearly putrid. These "messes" were to be eaten without knife, fork, spoon, or dish, unless the same were supplied by the prisoners themselves, which, fortunately, some of *our* number possessed; though knives had been taken away when we first boarded, but subsequently returned. A thick, coarse, hard, black biscuit, (not known in American shipping,) was also supplied, each day. We of course applied for a change of food; but all the benefit arising from the application was merely a permission to have our own tea made, and rice cooked, in lieu of the ship's provisions, providing we "would supply enough for the mess"; which, as a matter of necessity, we did; and the small sea stores we had providentially laid in, came in requisition, notwithstanding Frost's assertion. Some of the articles we had were of little use, such as Indian meal and flour, as the doctor, (cook) could seldom be induced to bake a cake or boil a pudding unless on the broad principle of a "full supply for all, agreeable to the Captain's orders". Almost enough has already been told, to excite, in the breast of every man, a feeling of contempt and hatred towards all who had anything to do with the management of that ship; and I can never feel otherwise than a profound abhorrence for them. Yet, I would say, in honor to Morton's humanity, that he did, after half the passage was done, permit the provisions, when supplied by the state prisoners, to be cooked distinct from the mess of the felons.

Poor L.W. Millar, chained to D. Deal, lay in a corner berth, on the opposite side of the ship, and almost shut from any of his countrymen; without murmur or complaint, passed several days without a particle of food passing his lips, having been too poor to purchase any, and too magnanimous to discover his necessity—it was discovered, however, and relieved. But, poor man, he was reduced to a mere skeleton, and we all felt a deep sympathy for him, though we were but a little better off.

It will not be supposed that I can give any description of our passage out the St. Lawrence. Indeed, I cannot; for we scarce saw day light, until after we had passed the grand bank; and all I can say, is, that the weather was high and the sea boisterous—that the decks, cordage, spars, and every thing about the ship, were covered with an immense quantity of ice; and that the Capt. feared much in consequence—that something was continually "giving away", and that most of the hands had some parts of their persons severely frozen—some of them in such a manner that they were rendered cripples for life. So great was the injury received by the extreme frost, that scarce men enough were left to work the ship. When we heard this information, we would have been eminently happy in offering our services to work the ship, and navigate her too.

This leads me into a relation of a scene that took place but two days after the foregoing information was received. Quite early, on the morning following the passing of the banks of New Foundland, an unusual bustle was observable on the deck; and Capt. Morton's voice was heard in calling "all hands on deck, even the cripples." Arms were supplied, and charged; and the men disposed so as to "be ready, in case of any rush from the hold; and when the order was given, to fire upon the prisoners." Such was the primary arrangement; and the next was, to come to our grate, and order all the men below into the berths, on pain of immediate death. The Captain then commanded Vernon and Mallery on deck, at the same time declaring that he was "armed to the teeth," and so were his men; and that they would "destroy every soul", if the slighest disposition to disobey, or move, was manifested among us. Then telling his men to cock their pieces, he hastily unlocked the grate, and drew out V. and M. with immense trepidation, and slammed back the door suddenly, as if a rush was expected from beneath. These movements astonished us, and we remained in suspense as to the meaning of the uproar, until they had brought the two men to the deck, when their vehemence got the better of their judgement; and in their haste to vent their wrath, the information was undesignedly conveyed to us. They accused the state prisoners of premeditating a mutiny, to take the ship, and sail into an American port. The two men actually had their chains nearly severed, while three other couple had theirs cut in two.

After considerable altercation, and a vain attempt to "seize Vernon to the mizzen rigging for a flogging," they were "turned below," without any elucidation, farther than the discovery of the tool, a notched knife, with which the chains had been cut. Parker and myself were next called up. For my part, observing their nervousness, I felt a little obstinate; and, consequently, passed up the companion ladder rather slowly, which they construed into an inclination to favor a rush after me, and drew me up with a roughness hardly consistent with kindness, and shut the door with a celerity that clearly proved fear reigning predominant with them. It was truly ridiculous to observe the precautions taken against a surprise from a few unarmed and manacled prisoners. I laughed outright, to see the master of the ship standing on the poop, with a pistol in each hand, and a "volunteer's hoop hilted sword" by his side, tremblingly agitated. The guard, and all the men on board, were fully armed, and peculiarly dispersed; some behind the main, the fore, and the mizzen masts, while others were in the boat, or behind casks, and all with their arms in an attitude of defence.

The master of the barque, and master of the guard, both at the same time, upbraided us with having planned a conspiracy against them, which, they declared they were informed, was to have broken out that day, headed by Parker and myself, whom they *swore*, should be punished with unmitigated "severity." "Cruelty, you mean," said I—"Yes, cruelty," M. replied. "But, then," I rejoined, "calmness is requisite, to enable you to make proper enquiry; and an investigation may prove your information erronous." "No! No!" he replied, "our information is correct; and you were using the saw on your chains, when we received it; and the mark will suffice to prove what I say. Will you permit me to have your chain examined?" "Most assuredly you can do that; but you ought to be careful how you hold those weapons in your hand, for they may prove dangerous to your friends, as well as to us, through your extreme agitation." This so exasperated him, that he swore, and fumed, and stamped, like a mad fellow. I felt in a provocative humor, and indulged it to his great annoyance, more particularly after the chain had undergone an examination, without the discovery they so confidently expected.

Dinner time being now arrived, we were sent down, and farther investigation deferred for the present. On the next morning, however, the bustle recommenced, with an order for Beemer and Van Camp to go to the deck, who were soon sent back again, when Parker and myself were called to undergo another ordeal. As soon as we got above, Morton accosted us with bitter invectives, and said he had positive evidence of our guilt, and was sure of finding the mark; if he did, our punishment should be exemplary. His scrutiny, this time, was crowned with the desired success; for he *really detected* our guilt, by discovering the small incision made in Montreal, by Gemmel, who, with Vernon, wore the chain at that time, as before stated.

I cannot say that I ever saw more frenzied delight, exhibited by any beings, than these men manifested. It seemed as though the very sluice gates of demoniac pleasure were unlocked; for now they had occasion, however trifling, for punishing the very men they so greatly feared, and whom they anxiously sought to terrify. He produced a large chain, weighing near half a hundred, and persisted in displacing the small one we wore, with it, notwithstanding the testimony of every Upper Canadian, and Mr. Gemmel, who nobly came to the grate, and declared he had made the incision in the manner before explained. I certainly did not bear this new indignity with very good temper, for I became exasperated in my turn, and told Morton I deemed his conduct *wantonly cruel*, and COWARDLY; and, although he could emit upon us his whole malignant rancor, as we were manacled, and in his power, *yet he should not do it with impunity*. We should yet meet on equal terms; and if it was twenty years hence, I would hold him to account for it, and require ample satisfaction.

I pitied his weak and dastard fears; and considered oppression of helpless beings, the sure indication of a mean and cowardly heart. He vindicated his conduct "on the score of the intended mutiny". But I told him, in strong terms, that he could not have attached any real blame to us, if we had risen, and even committed murder, in revenge for having been thrust into such an infamous hole, and starved and treated as we were. It appears this language was construed into a challenge, and carefully entered as such in his log, which was published by the owner as soon as the ship arrived in Liverpool, where credit was rendered "Capt. Morton, for his intrepid conduct, in discovering and suppressing a most dangerous mutiny, and the fearless manner in which he had visited the ring leaders with deserved punishment, while *he magnanimously pardoned* the others"; with a column of other bombast, where I came in for a full share of abuse. It is exceedingly strange, indeed, that we did not suspect Beemer as the informer; for circumstances were strong against him. We supposed it had originated in a petty quarrel with some of the felons, which were not unfrequent. But it was afterwards proved to have been him, as I will have occasion to relate.

> Oh! for a curse to kill the slave,
> Whose treason, like a deadly blight,
> Comes o'er the councils of the brave,
> And blasts them in the hour of might.

The large, heavy chain, it may well be imagined, added much to our misery. Mr. Parker generally stood by the side of the berth, so as to be under the light for reading, while I lay down at the same time, for the same purpose; the chain, therefore, hung over the side of the berth, with its whole weight on my ankle; and I can assure you, it caused no small pain and anguish, which I endured for ten or twelve days; when, being in sight of land, the Captain begged we would permit him to *divest* us of the large, and *invest us* with the small chain. I, at first, opposed the change, determined on calling the attention of the authorities to this outrage, immediately after landing; but Parker, desirous of escaping the obloquy such a difference in guards would undoubtedly attract, readily assented, well knowing that Morton could easily find means to evade any odium that might be attached to him on investigation. I finally consented too, and found some relief as my leg had swollen very much. For the last ten days of our passage, we were permitted to spend an hour, each day, on deck; and although the air was chill and raw it was a happy and comfortable hour. This one hour of fresh air, and free and wholesome breathing, did more towards reinvigorating our frames, than any thing else that could have been offered; and, indeed, I was grateful to God, but not to the Captain, for the enjoyment of it.

A Reverend gentleman, by the name of Osgood, had taken a cabin passage on board the same barque, for Liverpool, and frequently visited us in christian kindness—to pray, sing, and converse with us, which relieved the tedium of many an hour. He was a New Englander, and had seven times crossed the Atlantic, on holy missions to the poor and degraded of London; where he had spent, at one time, eighteen months of arduous toil in the service of his Master, subsisting upon sixpence sterling per day.

For the last ten days of the passage, Capt. Morton seems to have relented of his severity towards us; and, as if to reconcile Parker and myself, he especially allowed us to remain longer than the others, sometimes overcoming his fears sufficiently to detain us on the deck four hours, while others were coming up and going below in rotation; all the time, however, the guards were under arms, and kept strict watch. Morton appeared, naturally, a quiet, inoffensive sort of a man; but having arisen from before the mast, he was highly puffed up with the importance of his station. This opinion of himself, common with men of his country and class, connected with egregious cowardice, rendered him an intolerable despot.

During our passage out of the Gulf of St. Lawrence, and until we had passed the Grand Banks of New Foundland, the weather continued unchangeably cold and boisterous, but then became mild and moderate—in salubrity much like our April and May—yet, when we approached the Irish coast, it assumed a colder aspect, and the dampness rendered it far less endurable to us than the American severe, though clear and dry atmosphere.

Our entrance of the Mersey was cheerless; more particularly on account of the mist and fog so prevalent all over England, at that season of the year.

> I remain, dear sir,
> Yours, &c. &c.

8

LIVERPOOL

Ashgrove, near Oatlands, V.D.L.
December, 1840.

To ——,

My Dear Sir: —

After the expiration of twenty-five days, our passage across the Atlantic was completed, and our anchor cast in the river Mersey, three miles from Liverpool, on the 16th December, 1838—just thirty-eight days after leaving Fort Henry.

We were soon transferred to a small steam lighter, and conveyed to the city. We lay some time at the stupendous docks, where we had an opportunity of beholding, with wonder and admiration, the extent of those magnificent and greatly useful works of art, that have cost millions of treasure, and years of labor to complete. The tide was out, and we were many feet below the top of the quay, where was collected a vast multitude, betraying the utmost curiosity.

More favorable circumstances could not have well been afforded to test and learn the general feeling for us; for a detestation, if felt, must break out in insult and violent expressions; but, to their honor be it said, that not the slightest disposition of the kind was exhibited, except by a sooty little chimney sweep, with the equipments of his order in his hand. But, on the contrary, all was calm sympathy, with a few low murmurs of pity and commiseration running through the crowd, that was grateful to the ears of the wretched exile; and, when we were all standing upon "terra firma," the throng having opened a lane for us, there went forth one continuous peal, with "God bless the brave Canadians, and speedily release and return them to their wives and to their homes."

Before we landed, however, the Liverpool owner, with a number of magistrates, boarded us, followed by the Governor of the borough jail, and a man carrying a load of burnished hand cuffs, with which we were connected in parties of four—"felon style". In the street near the dock, a number of carriages were drawn up, into which we were put, and whirled away to the old borough jail— an immense building, erected exclusively for the detention of French prisoners taken on the continent, during the struggle with Bonaparte—but which was now devoted to the punishment of convicted criminals. It is said to be capable of accommodating upwards of a thousand persons. At the time of our entrance, there were, as I was informed by an officer belonging to the establishment, about five hundred men and boys and two hundred women. The boys were upwards of two hundred in number, and under the age of ten—all convicted of larceny, or felony of some degree—and under sentence of from six months to two years close imprisonment, on the silent system.

In entering this *palace,* our carriage was driven by a postillion, with a guard on the boot. The heavy gates closed violently after us, as if to preclude the idea of ever repassing its dark and gloomy portals. As we rattled up the paved court yard, beneath the frowning towers and grated windows, a melancholy satisfaction pervaded my whole soul; for it was indeed a pleasure to be, even thus, delivered from the loathsome habitation we had just left, though we entered a boding prison.

At the main entrance, we were obsequiously received by the officials; and I wondered if it was not deemed a privilege to become a tenant, where so kind and favorable a welcome was administered. It reminded me of the picture I had somewhere seen, of the quaint affability of a landlord, standing upon his threshhold, dispensing welcome to his guests, well knowing that every new visiter added to his gains. I am sure he might well be lavish in retailing his good wishes, when each was worth at least a half crown to him. The doors were immediately thrown wide, and we were *politely* handed from the carriage, into a long, narrow hall, lined, on either side, with a row of sleeping cells, whose heavy, iron bound doors, with grated diamonds, were not calculated to impress us with an idea of a repletion of comforts within. About half way up the hall, we turned a sharp angle, and soon emerged into a tolerably spacious yard, flagged with large flat stones, (as was the case with all the ground rooms, halls and yards of the building,) and flanked on the outer side, and separated from another yard, by heavy walls, fifteen or twenty feet high, with a coping stuck full of broken glass bottles, formidable enough, in appearance, to deter the stoutest heart from any attempt to pass over it. In this yard we remained until dispossessed of all our iron *embarrassments;* and I can assure you, that, at the moment, I felt not only light footed, but light hearted also. We were next ranked in single file, and addressed by the Governor, (Mr. Batcheldor,) who stated that Mr. Jeffries, of the Quebec jail, had forwarded documents to him, expressive of an exceeding good character, which he was glad to see, and hoped we would maintain it; "for", said he, "character, in this country, with a prisoner, is every thing, and it may be in my power to do you a good turn in that way." The "board of visiting magistrates", who were present, with the lord mayor, and ex-mayor, expressed a deep regard for us, and a willingness to do any thing in their power, to meliorate our situations, and add to our comfort. They told us the establishment was conducted upon the "silent system"; but that they would consider us exempt from an obedience to that rule. No tobacco, newspapers, or books of light literature, however, would be permitted; and no articles, of any kind, taken out from, or brought in to us—no letters, or written communications, should pass, unless first inspected by the Governor, who would always be ready to extend any favor compatible with rectitude—and if we felt ourselves aggrieved, in any respect, we only had to make it known to the board of visiting magistrates, some of whom would see us each day. All these things arranged, we were dismissed, and permitted to retire from the yard to the "day room," where we found an exhilarating fire, around which we hastily crowded, with grateful sensations, for once again being disencumbered from our galling load, and permitted to thaw our chilled bodies. The felons from Quebec remained outside still longer, and listened to a catalogue of crimes and "bad marks", that ought to have separated them for ever from all human society; nevertheless the lenient Governor would permit them to remain with us, on account of the whole number being *"in transitu"*; but he hoped they would not, in the least, interfere with us. When we had become comfortably placed, and felt the influence of the fire, (something we had been debarred from for twenty-five cold days past,) supper appeared, in the shape of a half pound of black barley and pea bread, and a three half pint cup filled with potatoes, and a small slice of meat on the top. This provision, though coarse, was partaken with avidity, when, "out of respect of our being men not stamped with henious offences", a pot of ale to each was served out; and much surprise was exhibited by several gentlemen who stood by, to observe some of our number refuse to partake it, from temperance principles, which their persuasions could not overcome. This supper was served us out of pure humanity; for it was a practice there or, rather, a standing rule throughout England's jails, to never supply food to the prisoners on the first day of their arrival, supposing them to have been rationed for the day at their last stopping place. This is a cruel rule, for prisoners in *transitu*, seldom receive their customary allowance; and never what nature would seem to require. To any appeals, the governors are always inflexible; and the poor, hungry wretch is never relieved, except some humane fellow prisoner, where he lodges, but little better supplied than himself, chance to share his scanty pittance with him, which, in the whole, would not satiate a common appetite.

In the persuasions used to induce an acceptance of the ale, we were told, that it was a peculiar favor granted by the Governor; and, if slighted, he might be offended. But all was to no purpose; for, had not pledged abstinence withheld us, I think a taste would have been sufficient; for I cannot conceive what there can be in this national beverage, to cause the English people to idolize it to such a degree—to an American palate it is perfectly nauseous.

Next came our sleeping apartments, to which we were shown about eight o'clock; upon these, my mind had been running for some hours past, for our last quarters had been so destitute of comfort, that we felt as though we ought to find something of a better kind here. We however soon discovered that they had been furnished with but little regard to comfort, yet with much regard to cleanliness, a very redeeming feature. The calculation was, for three to occupy a cell. Messrs. Wixon, Parker, and myself took one, and found three narrow cribs, very like coffins, with a mattress, two blankets, and a pillow, handsomely rolled up in each. And, although I had the precaution to take in my overcoat and cloak, yet I felt the necessity of more bedding. I really thought Mr. Wixon would never recover that night's severity; and I do not know that he ever has. He was seized with a violent dysentery, and could obtain no alleviation for the night. The morning came, and with it new scenes; for we were directed to roll our beds as we found them, clean our cribs, sweep the room, rub, with a white stone, the door sill, and carry out the nuisance tins—wash them in a large stone trough, standing beside a well in the yard; then pile them regularly in one corner of the yard. Next, we were to undergo ablution ourselves, in the same stone trough; and then rank, in single file, opposite a window opening into the main court, when breakfast made its appearance, consisting of the pots, (in which our suppers had been served,) filled with the detested oatmeal gruel and a half pound of the "brown tommy". My gruel, as well as many others, remained uneaten. After breakfast recourse was again had to the trough, to cleanse our *dishes.*

About an hour after we had breakfasted, two of the felons from another wing of the establishment, (both doing the term of their sentence there, the one a year for smuggling, the other eighteen months for vagrancy, alias, poaching) came to our apartment, to teach us the art of cleaning, scouring, and scrubbing it. The benches and tables that circled the whole ward, first underwent a scouring with sand and water, rubbing with half a cocoa nut; then cleaned with soap and water. The next was, to sweep and scrup the flagged floor, then to rub the whole with a white stone; and, lastly, the whole yard, an area of about one hundred feet by forty, was swept and mopped, and likewise the immense hall, which ended the labors for the day; and the orders were, that we should observe how it was done, so as to be able to do the same on the following morning. Out of the twenty-three state prisoners only four, (native Scotchmen,) could partake of the oat meal; and, consequently, several cups remained full, sitting on the table; when the felons came in, they looked so wistfully at them, that we could not misunderstand—we therefore told them to eat what they wanted. The poor, half starved wretches, actually emptied five cups each, and declared they had never enjoyed so ample a meal before.

The visiting magistrates soon made their appearance, and we at once applied for a change of the gruel, for something else more palatable. They complied, and granted milk in lieu thereof; but the bread they could not alter. With the magistrates came Mr. Thornby, M.P., the ex-mayor, and Lord Bishop, John Buck, D.C.L., Chaplain, and Dr. Archer, surgeon to the borough jail. They all spoke kindly, and encouragingly, and hoped we would not long remain in prison, but soon be permitted to return to our homes. They proffered every friendship, and said, "if you have good friends in America, you have equally good ones here, and those who will serve you more effectually." They further advised us to write any friends we might have in England, and bring ourselves, by that means, into notice. So many applications had already been made to see us, out of sheer curiosity, that it had become necessary to utterly close the door against all visitors.

Some of them, in the plenitude of their kind solicitude, advised us to abstain from communicating with Messrs. Hume, Roebuck, and others of that class, whose services would be rather detrimental than beneficial to our interests. They departed, and we felt pretty well satisfied with the reception our first request had met. But Dr. Buck remained behind, for further conversation; and pleased us much with the kind solicitude he manifested, and the apparent pleasure with which he deeply engaged in every thing appertaining to our temporal, as well as our spiritual welfare. This gentleman continued to visit us each day, and was exceedingly alive to every christian principle. His unbounded benevolence and generous attention, excited in each breast a sense of grateful pleasure, that never can be forgotten. In many subsequent scenes, when my whole soul has been wrung with oppression, and my mind driven to feelings of retribution against the human race, his character has stood out in *relief,* as a bright spot upon which I could gaze with satisfaction, and say there was *one good man!* Not a single trait of character was exhibited but what seemed governed and dictated by pure principles of christianity and universal love. I cannot relate a more expressive tribute to his philanthropy, than the following little incident that took place at his house, on the evening of our landing. It was usual for a select few of his friends to collect at his house occasionally for the purpose of social prayer and spiritual conversation. When engaged in one of these little bands, the news of our landing was conveyed to him. They instantly, at his suggestion, resolved to adopt our condition and ultimate release, as the absorbing subject of that night's prayers; and it was late 'ere those petitions ceased: the result was a strong hope of the interference of Providence in our favor; and he sought daily to infuse that *hope* into our minds. He had been engaged in the service of his country in the east, where he had, by intrepid conduct, worked his way from the ranks, up to the station of Major of Artillery, when he renounced the service of his country, for that of his divine Master—the uniform of a warrior, for the surplice—the sword of destruction, for the gospel of peace; and in this character he was preeminently useful, and had already attained the degree of Doctor of Civil Law. We gladly listened to his discourses and prayers, which were always extempore. He was an agreeable visitant to all who were desirous of instruction. He discovered an uncommon depth of thought, and delivered his sentiments with a readiness and eloquence that was truly fascinating. His understanding appeared remarkably clear, which was coupled to a quick apprehension, a solid judgement, and an excellent memory;

and was ardently devoted in promoting the worship of "Israel's Covenant God."

On Christmas he attended with his daughter, (a child of about eight years,) in his hand, who had been long anxious "to come and see the poor Canadians". When I beheld the dear sympathizing creature holding to her parent's hand, gazing upon us with a tearful eye, (for she had been taught to pity us,) and enquiring of our own dear little ones, strong emotions of bitter regret were excited in my bosom. The picture brought vividly to my recollection, scenes of the past; contrasting what was and what might have been my situation. I then felt, more than ever, the severity of the fiat that had rent asunder the sweet ties of domestic society, and the friendships that still bound my heart to the land of my birth. Although scenes of this nature would cause my thoughts to revert, sadly, to my home; yet gloom could not endure—it would vanish at the idea of having one *friend*, who would not, while life lasted, cease her struggles to emancipate, or join me in my land of exile. And it was a melancholy pleasure, too, to know I had left behind a daughter to bless the name of her absent parent, and who would ever be taught to pray for his release and return.

Our first dinner consisted of a half pound of bread, and a pint of "scouse, made of cows heads", boiled to a jelly with lips and gullet yet covered with the provender the beast had last eaten—the second of a cup of beef broth or "beef tea," as it was called, with the usual bread, and half a pound of beef; and the third of the same as the first supper. These dinners came in perpetual rotation, while the breakfasts and suppers consisted, after the change, of one pint of milk each.

We were in the heart of a foreign prison, four thousand miles from home —shut from society, friends, and enjoyments—debarred the opportunity of action, and the commonest privileges of the free—without a hope of clandestine escape—with but a faint earnest of sympathy, and refused wholesome and proper provision: yet I do believe every man felt contented, cheerful, nay, even happy, for the contrast between the situation we had just left on board the Capt. Ross, and the one we occupied in the borough jail, was so great that it caused sensations of pleasure, grateful to feelings so long outraged: and when night came, we retired to our scanty beds, with strong anticipations of refreshing slumbers, and ideas of tolerable comfort.

Not withstanding the advice against writing Messrs. Hume, Roebuck, &c. I addressed them both, with Lord Brougham, for myself and the other Niagara District prisoners, as a distinct class. Messrs. Wixon and Parker did the same, representing their cases connectedly, with all from the London District and Toronto, who had taken the benefit of an "ex-post facto" law. Such proceedings were most justly represented as glaringly illegal, and most egregiously irregular; and Mr. Millar, on the part of the American citizens, wrote Mr. Stevenson, the U.S. Minister at the Court of St. James. In my letters I desired to hear "from some of those liberal spirits, who had so long stood up in the British Parliament, as the unbiased champions of reform, and the undaunted opposers of an evil, iniquitous ministry. I appealed on the score of fellow feeling, and earnestly solicited their aid, in bringing our cases before the eye of the government, so that, in the event of our sentences being carried fully into effect, there might be no ground upon which the British ministry could get rid of the onus of an illegal transportation; for, in Upper Canada, there never had existed any law, even recognising such an event, until but three months prior to our trial, when a bill was passed, only *anticipating* it; and that bill had not yet received the sanction of the Queen; and it was, therefore, unconstitutional to act upon it. But all the practices in the Province, were rife with unconstitutionality; yet, I fancied, there existed more responsibility in England, and, consequently, I imagined my appeal would not be vain." In fact when I first put my foot on British soil, I felt almost assured that I should not leave it, unless I was really *homeward bound.* I named, too, the *ruse* of Sir George Arthur, in entering into a compact with the prisoner, by which he could set up, against merited censure, the plea of the prisoner making choice of transportation in the lieu of death—a plea I regarded as perfectly puerile, and could only have originated in a total absence of all law upon a subject of the nature; and one that could not give the slightest coloring of propriety to such a violation of what was right, and I doubted not but that, if we could obtain a hearing, through such men as Brougham, Hume, and Roebuck, we would find liberality sufficient in the government, to release us from imprisonment, if not a full permission to return to our residence in Canada.

To talk of clemency, as connected with the Queen, I knew to be hyperbolical; for very rarely did any communications, designedly made for her, ever meet the eye of majesty, particularly when not agreeable to ministers through whose hands they must proceed. Ours, for instance, must be addressed to the Secretary of State for the Colonies, under whose arbitrary policy, explained to the Canadian Governor, it was that we were suffering. Even should these documents approach the throne, and elicit feelings of sympathy, yet they could not be acted upon, at her instance, if counter to the views of the ministry. Nevertheless, that there might be no "stone left unturned", I wrote out, and addressed to Lord John Russell, a petition, signed jointly by all my class, praying "Her Majesty's interference against an illegal sentence"; and boldly describing the means resorted to by the Lieutenant Governor to effect our transportation from the land of our homes. We ingeniously acknowledged having engaged in acts that might bear the construction of high treason; but in reality, it was not treason in us; we had merely opposed, by the only means remaining to us, the treasonable practices of Her Majesty's representative. We had lost many of the privileges and rights the constitution had provided for, and we only sought to retrieve them. "We had been driven to the measures we took", and I quoted Lord Durham to sustain it. "We protested against our inordinate bondage, and appealed to the justice and good will of her Majesty to her loyal subjects, for an effectual release, or, at least, an impartial investigation, &c. &c.; and lastly, we knew that when her Majesty became acquainted with our unhappy situation, and read our faithful representations, and listened to our appeals to her sense of equity, she *would* grant our petitions; and, as in duty bound, we would ever pray."

I next wrote Lord Durham, expressive of my personal gratitude for his forbearance, through the application of Mrs. Wait; and congratulated him on having "brought home so many testimonials of his good government, of which I was a living one." I recapitulated the substance of our paper to the Queen, and begged he would put in her hands all the documents he had received relative to my case, personally. I depended much upon the light he would throw upon Canadian affairs, and hoped he would make such representations, relative to our cases, as a politically oppressed people, that would result to our ultimate good; and "his liberal principles, connected with his unbounded influence, would, I am sure, be as effectual in procuring our liberation, as it had been in saving my life."

But all my expectations from him were vain! for all the answer I received, was a mere acknowledgement of my flattering note," and "an acquiescence in the request of placing at the disposal of the ministers, all the papers bearing upon the cases of sentenced political offenders;" and he, "at present, was not in a position to command any influence for, or call the attention of the Queen to them." Whatever Lord Durham's position was at that time, it is now an acknowledged fact, that his able report, that made its appearance in the House of Lords, but a short time subsequent to our leaving England, has done a deal of good to the oppressed people of the Canadas: and I sincerely hope he will receive his reward in the world to come; for I am sure he never will at the hands of his unwise and impolitic sovreign. The following extracts from a letter I received from Joseph Hume Esq. which gave considerable cause for exultation and encouragement.

Bryanston Square, 24th Dec. 1838.

"Sir: I have, on my return from the country, this moment received your letter of the 22d instant.

"I cannot hold out to you, or your unfortunate companions in misfortune, any hopes that I can do you any good; but I write to acknowledge your letter, and to say, that your cases shall immediately be inquired into.

"If you have a copy of your petition to the Queen, send me one, and such other information as may make me acquainted with your cases.

"In haste, I am your obd't serv't.
JOSEPH HUME,

"Mr. Benjamin Wait, Liverpool Borough Jail,

"P.S. Let me know whether this reaches you!!"

The above was soon followed by a note from Mr. W. Waller, who represented himself as having come from W.H. Ashurst, Esq., of London, Barrister and Solicitor to John Arthur Roebuck, Esq.—that his errand to Liverpool was, to see us, and obtain information for them; but not having brought an especial order to that effect, he could not obtain admission to our prison, until it came from the Secretary of State, for which he had since written. He also sent in a paper, purporting to be an agreement with W.H. Ashurst, to act as our solicitor, by which his services would be ensured, under the eye of Roebuck, Brougham, Hume, &c. The document was readily signed by all but Beemer, and returned. An order for his admission arrived; and, although seven in the evening, he came in, immediately, to inform us, that Mr. Roebuck would, himself, be down on the following day; and he suggested the propriety of appointing a person from each class, to confer with him, to avoid confusion. Messrs. Wixon and Parker, were to take precedence for their cases; and myself and Millar were to follow, for ours. It was arranged that Mr. Waller should introduce the four to Mr. Roebuck, while the others were to seek amusement in the yard. The next day, about four P.M. Mr. Roebuck made his appearance, accompanied by Mr. W. I was named to him; he acknowledged the receipt of my letter, and said, his design for coming, was to procure material sufficient to bring our cases into the Queen's Bench, which he had no doubt, would result favorably. His attention was then arrested by Mr. Parker's saying, that his class was not as deeply implicated as Mr. Wait's; and, perhaps; it might be better to bring their cases up first; as the one party had received a trial, and the other had not. Mr. Roebuck caught the idea at once, and desired to be left alone with him. They remained closeted for some time, when he took his leave without farther notice than merely saying, he had received all the information he desired, and would attend to the cause immediately—that he was cramped for time, and Mr. W. would inform me of the arrangements made; and requested that all the communications might be addressed to Mr. Ashurst.

I have been thus particular in relating these incidents, for my companions from Niagara, were inclined to charge the exclusive proceedings that followed, to the designed misrepresentations of Parker, and a fear that his success might be jeopardised by a too numerous participation in the benefits of inquiry; but I saw, at once, the occasion for it.

The nine men, among whom he was numbered, had been treated more palpably illegal, than those of us who had received a trial. Their sentences were given under an "ex post facto" law, directly opposed to the spirit of the British code, that nominal "bulwark of British liberty," viz: the "jury act." Ours, too, was illegal and unjust, but truly not so undisguised; for, by the time we were captured, Sir George Arthur had become somewhat more way-wise, and began to think a little more plausibility was requisite in dealing with the Canadians, than with the Tasmanians, whom he had hung up with impunity.

I was informed by Mr. Waller, that it had been determined upon to apply for a habeus corpus, under which twelve persons were to be taken to London for investigation and special pleadings before the Queen's Bench, while the others must still remain in the custody of the government; and all I could advance against such a fatal arrangement availed nothing. However, whatever induced our common friends to raise this distinction, I am quite certain it resulted detrimentally to the excluded party; for it created, in the estimation of the government, unfavorable impressions regarding our cases—the ministry naturally viewing this partial proceeding, as a tacit acknowledgement of a total want of all ostensible pretext for demanding a similar investigation and favor for us; yet, to keep up appearances, we were all desired to commit the particulars of each individual case to paper. For such purposes, paper, ink and quills, were gratuitously supplied by some without, who kindly sympathised with us.

We all, by advice, unitedly demanded copies of the official documents, under which we had been brought to, and were still detained in Liverpool. A dozen copies were taken without delay, and given us. It was a most singular instrument indeed, a mere warrant, drawn up and signed by John Colborne, Governor *pro tem.* of Lower Canada, Commanding Capt. Digby Morton, Master of the barque "Capt. Ross," to receive on board, and carry into transportation, the persons therein named—first landing them where "we" (the Queen) might deem proper, in the United Kingdom, "to the intent that they may be delivered into the hands of some person duly authorised to receive them."

The loose, vague, and slovenly manner in which this document was drawn up, elicited many pertinent remarks and observations from our counsel, and some public journalists. Perhaps a more decrepit instrument had never emanated from the pen of any individual who held the least pretensions to legal knowledge. The "recitation, (the only place in which we see Arthur named,) is extremely deficient in point of information. The reader can, in no wise, discover how the prisoners came into Colborne's possession, or by what authority he detained them." It all appears a matter of mere speculation, when first taken up, and so it leaves it. In the recitation, Leonard Watson's name is given, but does not again appear, although all the others (for one warrant *covered* the whole of us) are named six successive times. Had there been no other irregularity, the defective construction of this precept should have been sufficient reason for an immediate release. But, with the British government, *"might is right"*; and no justice is granted to the obnoxious, feeble bondsman notwithstanding the greatest inordinate practice.

I remain, dear sir,
Yours, &c. &c.

Ashgrove, near Oatlands, V.D.L.
January, 1841.

To ——,

My Dear Sir: —

I closed my last with some remarks concerning the instrument that bore the title of a warrant, and had the honor of taking twenty-three political prisoners from Canada to Europe. It only required reading, to be ridiculed, even by the comparatively illiterate. In fact, not only ridiculed, but also condemned, as placing unbounded authority in a petty master of a lumber ship, to deal with us as his disposition might dictate; and heaven is a witness, that his conduct bore no shade of humanity.

He, accompanied by the Liverpool owner, called upon us, and apologised for the publications relative to the mutiny. To show their regard, Mr. Frost, would undertake to forward free, any letters we might wish to send to America; as a packet, with which we had some connection, was about to sail for Boston. We accepted his proffer, and put in his hand a large number, which he sent on board the Pennsylvania and St. Andrews, two packets that went down in the channel; and with them all our letters.

Christmas, the great English feast day came, and brought to us the double rations usually issued in all their prisons; but we cared but little for their extras, for we had obtained the permission of making up a sort of mess, or pudding, from the relics of our sea stock. Flour, supplied by J.G. Parker, was mixed into dough, with *pure* water, then incorporated with a portion, still remaining, of the dried fruit sent me while yet at Kingston by a kind sister. This simple lump boiled, constituted our excellent Christmas dinner; and we partook of it with as hearty a relish as we would have done, of the choicest at home.

I mention this trifling incident, because it gave rise to a conversation upon the subject of England's paupers to which I listened with silent horror. While we were engaged with our "plum pudding," a gentleman who was always a privileged visiter, came in, and remarked, that he was happy to find us so well employed.

"But," said he, "you find your dinner, no doubt, a coarse one; and, perhaps, the poorest, in your country, would feel themselves poor, indeed, if they were not able to provide a better, any day in the year. But let me assure you, that there are millions, in this land, who never know what a full dinner is, even of the coarsest food— who seldom taste of meat—and, during the winter months, never partake of but one meal per day; and that, perhaps, but a half one. In the course of my duty, I have visited families who had not tasted food for days; and knew not where to turn for any. A famine is now raging in Manchester, that must very soon result in riot, blood-shed and murder, unless proper means are resorted to, to alleviate the prevalent misery and destitution. In fact the paupers of our whole land, are in a state but little better than starvation. There are none, perhaps, who witness so much human wretchedness, as the Clergyman, if he holds himself bound to attend the couch of sickness, and administer the consolations of religion to the dying, in their last moments. And, alas! what a harrassing task it is, to fulfil the duties of such a station! How often must his heart be torn by the scenes of anguish he beholds in the sheds of the starving poor! He finds it impossible to lead the mind of the expiring, to the consideration of a future state, when his children, (mere shadows of humanity,) are mourning about him for bread. How often must he rob his own dear ones of half their wants, to administer a slight comfort to the victim of aristocratic avarice; and even then, incur the charge of dealing out with a *cold handed charity*. The oppression of the many, for the aggrandizement of the few, is what has branded England with infamy. It is want! cold, meager, maddening, want! that causes so many of England's subjects yearly to overleap the barrier to crime, and become thieves, incendiaries, robbers and murderers. It is hunger! cruel, infuriating hunger! that fills our jails, penitentiaries, and hulks to overflowing, and has peopled, with abandoned outcasts, the penal colonies to which you are sentenced. I have more pity for that man, who suffers the extreme penalty of the law for high way robbery, if it was but to supply his needy offspring with food, than for him who rolls, in his splendid equipage, to a sudden end of horror.

"When I see the gaudy trappings of rank, and splendor, of riches, contrasted with the poor, forlorn beggar, in his tattered garments, and bare feet, with his gray locks streaming in the winds of winter, and his fleshless, trembling limbs, scarce bearing him up against the blasts, I cannot close my eyes upon the fact, that these are sure indications of a state of society, that must be charged for anarchy and bloodshed. If France has suffered much on account of her high-handed oppression, will not England suffer a thousand times more? But her measure is not yet full.

"Liverpool is more free from the wretched victims of inanition, than, perhaps, any other considerable city of the United Kingdom, yet our jails, (two extensive edifices,) do not afford room for near the whole number of petty criminals. This building, alone, contains upwards of three hundred adult males, and two hundred females; one half of whom have no other incentive for the commission of crime, than ostensibly to supply themselves and families with food. Two hundred boys occupy a portion, also; many of whom are under the age of eight, committed invariably for theft; and in five out of six cases, they have been inducted into the practices, by their own parents, frequently with a view to their entrance here. These little villains would surprise you, by their agility in getting possession of property, and their ingenuity in secreting it; their acuteness is indeed worthy a better cause.

"Such tales are scarcely to be credited, but they are true; and misery and crime will still, as they have been for past years, be on the increase, until our impolitic government devises some means to provide comfort and less dependance for her six millions of paupers. Man must be supplied with food, necessary clothing, and a proper share of intelligence, before crime will decrease.

"Our nation is daily adding to her stores of knowledge, science, art, and individual wealth; but the upper grade, alone, profit by them. Though the means of knowledge are as abundant as the bread stuffs the soil produces, yet they are to the poor, still more difficult to command. Has not England, in her small circle, more truly wretched than all the remainder of Europe. Has she not more infamy and crime gazetted in one year, than America in ten? Then why say that she is the most honored and wealthy nation in the world? In this *right merrie Ould Englande*—the land of matchless beauty—of uncommon production—renowned for hilarity, pleasure, generosity, charity, and philanthropy—the richest, most powerful, intelligent, and *free* in the universe—there are thousands dying yearly, from inanition—thousands rendered cripples, and truly hideous in appearance, by being, while too young, driven, in a starving condition, to labor incessantly, for twelve or fourteen hours per day, at the mills or factories, in a painful attitude, to which they inevitably fall victims at a premature age—millions, who know not what it is to use a single article of comfort—thousands, whose countenances, from continued destitution, settle down into a melancholy dejectedness; and whose spirits know no hilarity or pleasure—whose wants have never been relieved by the high sounding charitable, generous, sympathetic, or philanthropic gentry of the age! Millions, who are in the midst of riches, but dare not partake, and die, famished, in the sight of tuns of bread stuffs. It is true, England is powerful, because despotic! But *freedom* is dececrated by being coupled with her present institutions, which all tend to oppress the many, and pamper the few.

"I would not wish to be understood as saying that there are none whose necessities are relieved by private charity, or charitable institutions; for there are millions who do yearly receive the miserable pittance of eight or twelve pence per week, during the winter. But what is such a sum, in comparison to the wants of a human being, in a country where bread is so dear? I will not say that the 'abominable corn laws' produce all the misery prevailing here, but I cannot but admit, that they conduce largely towards it. Perhaps you do not know their operation; I will, therefore briefly explain it: wheat now, including the duty, ranges near $2.22 per bushel; and such is rendered continual by the sliding scale of rates, which rises, as wheat falls in value, and falls as wheat rises. Now, the great evil is, that this duty does not find its way into the treasury, but into the pockets of the great landlord.

"I say, the millions are starved, to gratify the few. Sir Robert Peel says, 'it is the constitutional policy of England to maintain the aristocracy and magistracy, as essential parts of the community;' and that 'the present evils are beyond Parliamentary enactment.' Official and newspaper reports of the day, say that, at least one half the deaths taking place among the lower class, are caused by a want of proper nutriment!! Can we wonder, then, that mobs, riots, and chartist meetings are so common? Nay, I am only astonished that bloodshed and murder are not more frequent! That every pauper is not a thief, robber, or incendiary; for at least one half the applicants, at the numerous workhouses, and charity and philanthropic institutions, are turned away unrelieved.

"Oh, how saddening to the better feelings of man—how shocking to the delicacy of nature, is the knowledge, that to the arbitrary policy of England, is attributable nearly all the immolations of our country women upon the shrine of prostitution, and consequent drunkenness, disease, and death. What will not starvation do? We have seen it sacrifice virtue and honor, to infamy, degradation, and vice—make the staid and sober citizen a robber, an incendiary! The moral man a monster in crime a murderer! The bold, laughing peasant, a sneaking, villainous fiend! The loving husband, and fond father, a demon, a homicide! The patient, devoted mother, an unnatural being, a horrid infanticide! and a virtuous, intelligent, and benevolent community, is changed into a suspicious, illiberal, atheistical, degraded, and criminal band!"

After listening to the foregoing tales, or rather conversation, upon "woful subjects", I laid down to rest, upon my hard couch, inclined to murmur *less*, at what I too well deemed hard treatment and ill fare; I was distracted with the idea that thousands of fellow-beings might be then vainly seeking a fevered rest on the bare ground, or expiring through want, within the same city. I could imagine I saw the distortion of their countenances, and heard their dying groans, though they were *free* and ostensibly protected by that *powerful* government which held me in thraldom. I remembered, too, the dreary manner in which I had spent the night previous to the last anniversary, in making my escape from Canada, across the broad and sweeping current of the Niagara, on a log canoe, that would scarcely float, when I nearly fell a victim to frost and extreme cold. I slept soundly, and dreamed of all I had heard, and a thousand additional horrors, and awoke to a knowledge of my own unhappy condition, with a keen sense of the loneliness and unprotected situation of my wife and child. And if I ever prayed with fervor, in my life, it was then, for their well-being, and exemption from want and misery. I more than ever deprecated the idea of Mrs. Wait's coming to England, and wrote positively prohibiting it; but that letter, too, was lost, with the Pennsylvania.

The time was now coming in which we were to embark for Portsmouth. I therefore made another effort to prevent, or, rather, show the fallacy of creating the distinction, and excluding a part of the prisoners from investigation. I explained to Mr. Waller, that I had great misgivings upon being sent to the hulks; assuring him, that I felt certain, that when placed on them, there would be no probability of leaving, until sent on the transport ship—that I had heard so much about the horrors of those "floating prisons," that I dreaded a residence there, more than immediate transportation. He was very anxious to convince me that it was "only nervousness", and we had no reason to be under apprehensions concerning the treatment we should receive; as he would take care that a proper agent should be appointed, in Portsmouth, to attend to our wants. In fact, one had already been employed; and he gave me the address of J.W. Greetham, Esq., barrister, &c.; then added, "if you find your abode less agreeable than you can reasonably expect, you have only to make it known to W.H. Ashurst, Esq. barrister, 137 Cheap side, London, and he will remove you by 'habeas corpus', is there is the least probability of any benefit resulting." I said, I had no doubt but that the government, since our friends had admitted a distinction, would avail themselves of it as a pretext for sending us away; for the fact of being sent to a hulk without protest, would, on our part, be an acknowledgement of its legality; and that we considered ourselves still "in transitu", merely awaiting an opportunity of being conveyed on the voyage. Indeed, those prison ships were only regarded as receptacles for men whose cases were positively decided; therefore, being sent there, was significant enough of what the government designed doing with us; consequently, I felt it a duty to draw up a protest against a removal, intimating that if we yielded at all, it would be on the ground of *expediency*. This paper was presented at the Queen's Bench, when the Attorney general pledged his honor, "that, although the government views them as being *in transitu*, none should be sent away until each has his case thoroughly investigated." Mr. W. promised to do what he could, to effect a removal to London, of the whole number; but he feared it would be impracticable; "as the moment a man is placed under a *habeas corpus*, the expense of his support falls upon those who obtain it." Indeed! the secret was out, and I said no more. I had repeatedly been informed, the feeling was so strong in our favor, that should our liberation be offered on indemnity or bail, either would be immediately forthcoming. Then, it was not philanthropy, but political partisanship, that had dictated an interference at all! I therefore made no farther struggle to prevent the removal; and twice, subsequently, refused to permit my name to be added to those going to London, and thus be separated from my fellows, whose cases were so closely joined to mine by similitude.

The vessel, destined to convey us to Portsmouth, arrived; but a clashing between the orders brought by her, and some that had come by land, caused a short delay. In the mean time, many gentlemen of the city exhibited a great anxiety to administer to our comfort, or show their esteem, by some slight token; but all the Ministry would permit us to receive, was a supply of shoes, to all who needed them; but few, however, were required; consequently, the Niagara prisoners went away without having been much expense to these philanthropists. The debt of gratitude due to Dr. Buck was augmented by the present of a volume of evangelical hymns, got up by himself, in a splendid style, most of them original. Mine was bound in a superb manner, and I still retain it as a valuable memento of his christian regard.

On the first of January, we were favored with sociable visits from various gentlemen; and many ladies made application, in vain, to be admitted. However, they were not to be utterly thwarted, and sent for me to the grated door, having read or heard of Mrs. Wait's successful application at Quebec. I found a considerable number collected, and had the honor of a short conversation with one who had been a "Lady Mayoress." They were all very richly attired, and betrayed the utmost curiosity and sympathy, as well as an immense degree of ignorance upon Canadian matters and inhabitants. The conversation turned, of course, upon my wife's conduct; and I felt high pleasure in listening to their comments. Indeed, they were extravagant; and *promised* "as great success to her endeavors, as the most ardent mind could anticipate, if she really did come to England;" and should she land in Liverpool, she should have their protection and assistance, in every possible shape; and I might be assured that would not be slight. They received my gratitude with a few paper mementoes, and retired from the door, leaving me to return to the enjoyment of my prison associates.

But here I will close, and bid you adieu.

> I remain, dear sir,
> Yours, &c. &c.

9

LIVERPOOL TO PORTSMOUTH

Ashgrove, near Oatlands, V.D.L.
February, 1841.

To ——,
My Dear Sir: —
I believe my last letter ended with a scene at the door of the Liverpool borough jail, between some *curious* ladies, and your equally curious humble servant. The assurances they gave me, of extending the kind hand of protection and assistance to my bereaved wife, in case of her landing there, did my heart good; and made me regret having thus hastily written to her so disparagingly of the attempt; for these sympathetic feelings satisfied me, that the object of her mission, and the generosity and benevolence of her motives, would ensure her an enthusiastic reception. I do not know as I have ever received any expressions, that have sent to my heart a greater thrill of pure delight, or sensations of more grateful pleasure, than that very trifling scene. It was, in my mind, the very harbinger of her success; and it did more than all else, to determine me to bear up under every succession of misfortune that might approach me.

The following is a copy of what was entered into the diary of J.G. Parker, for January 4th. 1839, copied and inserted since my return.:

At daylight the rattling of chains announced to us, that the eleven prisoners were being prepared to embark for Portsmouth. Their chains were riveted on them, as well as on the eleven convicts from Quebec. After dinner they went on board—Dr. Buck having previously prayed with us—and the separation was affecting, as their leaving was under apprehension that they should not see us again. Dr. Buck saw them on board the Meteor, (which is but a small vessel,) and the Governor spoke to the Captain of the steamer of the good conduct of the prisoners while in his custody. After the twenty-two persons were gone, we felt quite lonesome.

Indeed, the "separation was affecting;" for when we had been reinvested with our old acquaintances, and ranked up for a start, those who were to remain behind, (Messrs. Wixon, Watson, Parker, Bedford, Malcolm, Brown, Alves, Walker, Anderson, Miller, Grant, and Reynolds,) lined the hall near the door of our egress, with Dr. Buck at their head, they wrung our hands with tearful eyes, and many a "God bless you," while they assured us they would correspond with, and inform us of what passed with them, *if permitted.* The generous Dr. in his usual bland, affectionate manner, strove to direct our minds "to strong hopes in, and firm reliance on Israel's covenant God, who would relieve the weary soul, and release the confiding prisoner." He shook our only unshackled hand (for handcuffs, as before had been replaced with the chains,) and put in mine, a pocket comb, which I still retain, as a sacred memento of the "one good man". He also gave me a letter of commendation,* that has frequently, since, been the cause of considerable respect and ameliorating circumstances. Carriages awaited us at the door, into which we got, and were treated with a drive through the fine city, in view of splendid edifices, down to the dock where the "Meteor" a small steam frigate lay ready to receive us.

It was about half-past three P.M. when we embarked, and were conducted to the bow cabin, just vacated by the marines, where we found all our baggage, with a bed each, wooden trencher bowl and spoons. Dr. Buck, and Mr. Bacheldor, (the governor) with the commander came in immediately when we were counted, and a list of our names given. The Governor reported an extraordinary character for the state prisoners, and recommended them to the especial favor of the officers—then bid us a pleasurable passage, and speedy release from imprisonment, and retired. The Dr. again imparted excellent advice, and bid us adieu, with a parting prayer.

About 6 P.M. the steam was got up, moorings loosed, and the frigate put under way for the sea, against a head wind, by which we were twice forced back before we made good our offing. The morning of the fifth,

---

*   Liverpool Borough jail,
                                    December 28, 1838.

Dear Sir:—

I can have no difficulty in expressing my approbation of the conduct evinced by you, and the other prisoners, while you have been unhappily confined within these walls.

I trust you will have that support which true religion can alone afford you; and that, wherever your lot may be cast, you will ever realize Israel's Covenant God. I most affectionately commend you to the grace of God, and to the Christian sympathy of my brethren in the ministry whom you may meet. My prayers and my best wishes for yourselves, your wives, and your children.

                              Believe me yours, very respectfully,
                              John Buck, D.C.L. Chaplain

Mr. Benjamin Wait
& Messrs. McLeod, Wait, Waggoner, Candler,
Gemel, McNulty, Vernon, Mallery, Cooley,
Van Camp, and Beemer.

found us almost a wreck, laboring heavily in an increased gale, off Cork harbor, which we attempted, but found impracticable, after the whole day spent fruitlessly. The commander then deemed it necessary to bear away from Holyhead, where we rode off and on for the night, not daring to enter without a pilot; and signals for one in the morning, were only answered by counter signals to keep off. Our case was now desperate, and every moment becoming worse; the engine was disabled and stopped; the wheel houses, bulwarks, binacles and compasses were all swept away; the boats were destroyed, and no chance left for escape, but to run again for Liverpool, under almost bare poles; for but one sail was remaining, the others having been shredded to ribbons by the force of the wind.

It was, indeed, no easy matter to re-enter Liverpool, without a single channel mark, buoy, or light, to guide our course; all having been displaced, and the light ship driven in; but there was no alternative; the commander took the wheel and drove for the mouth of the Mersey, guided by the wrecks that lined each bank of the channel, shown by the vivid lightning's gleam, that at intervals exhibited the fell destruction that surrounded us. The night was otherwise excessively dark and murky. At length, near midnight on the 7th we re-entered the river, and cast anchor opposite the city, almost a complete wreck, after having encountered such imminent danger, and witnessed so many wrecks and deaths.

During the three days and two nights we were thus "riding the gale," our cabin was utterly darkened; the large skylight being canvassed over and battened down; which, however, did not exclude the water that at every succeeding wave poured down upon us in torrents, and not only drenched us, but set our beds afloat, the cabin deck being our only berths. Not a man among us was free from violent sea sickness. Our situation can be easier imagined than described; and it may readily be conceded that we needed, or, at least, received, no food during these days of misery. It is, indeed, hard to *conceive* the wretched appearance we made, when we first emerged from that sink, and the horrid stench that arose from the cabin, when the sky light was first unbattened. The marines who did it, swore they never had experienced anything half so nauseous. Yet no blame could be attached to the commander or any of the officers; for it would scarcely be supposed that they could pay much regard to us, when the whole ship, lives, and every thing, were in such imminent jeopardy. Much credit is even due them, for their intrepid management; and endless gratitude is due the Almighty, for again bringing us to port through every vicissitude and suffering, while many ships were wrecking, and hundreds of fellow creatures were sinking to a watery grave in our sight.

On going on board, McLeod was my *yoke-fellow*; but we were soon separated, in consequence of my ill health; and the chains were taken off my leg entirely. My complaint was a chronic one, the virulence of which, at that time, was augmented by a pulmonary attack; and when we returned to port, the marine surgeon deemed it necessary to have assistant advice. Dr. Archer, therefore, came on board, accompanied by another medical gentleman, who proceeded to examine my chest, breast, and sides, with a stethescope, and pronounced it necessary to remove me to the shore, where I might join my other companions, and go to London by land. This advice arose from a benevolent anxiety to befriend me, and I thanked them for it, but declined accepting, from a wish to remain with, and share the fortune of my present companions, knowing that my services, in writing, would soon be necessary.

Dr. Buck came off, also, and brought a slip from one of the presses, containing a detail of many of the wrecks, with the loss of life and destruction of property, on shore, as well as at sea.

The Pennsylvania and St. Andrew's Packets, bound for America, filled with emigrants and passengers, were stranded, and went to pieces—only one man being saved from the P., while of the passengers on the St. Andrews, more, providentially, were preserved. The Brothers, and Lockwood, two others Packets, just entering the channel, shared the same fate, with nearly all their crews and passengers, while a vast number of smaller crafts were totally swallowed up, with all hands, involving the destruction of an immense amount of property, and the loss of several hundreds of human lives. The east shore of the channel was literally strewn with dead bodies, goods and property and pieces of wrecks. The detail was shocking, to a painful degree; and, although our own escape had been indeed a miraculous one, when I finished reading there was not a dry eye among us, nor a heart that did not bleed for the misfortunes of others. From one of the wrecks some of the passengers were taken by a life boat, and many drowned in attempts to escape. One gentleman refused, when an opportunity offered, to leave the ship, because his wife could not be found—choosing rather to stay and die with her, than to live, uncertain of her fate. He found her, and they both spent a night of horrors, in momentary expectation of death; but were, providentially both found alive on the following morning, the only surviving beings on board. There was true, genuine, close attachment, equal to other I wot of. A father and son were found on the beach, clasped in each other's arms—a husband, wife, and daughter, lashed together with handkerchiefs and shawls—a brother and sister in a last enduring embrace; and mothers and children were found as if they had clung to each other in vain for mutual protection. The picture was replete with horror and heart-rending sensations; but, ah! how many thousand times more lamentable must the real spectacle have been. The devastation was not confined to the channel and sea; for much of the shipping in the harbour and docks suffered material damage, while many lives, and much property were destroyed in the city of Liverpool, and the adjacent country, by the total demolition of thousand of chimneys, steeples, and even houses. Many stately elms, that had braved the storms of past ages, were torn up by the roots and thrown to the earth, terrible tokens of the force of the tornado, that had never, on those coasts, its parallel. Alas! the mutability of all things earthly! After some essential repairs, we again hoisted anchor, with a tolerable merry "yo-heave-o," and put out, with a gentle breeze, though high sea, about noon of the 11th. of January.

The contrast between this egress from, and the last entrance to the harbor, was truly very great. Then, the whole firmament was darkened with the fearful gale, and nothing but scenes of devastation were visible; but now the sun shone brightly out, and our gallant little frigate rode calmly onward, as if there had been no gloomy convulsions, no frightful dangers, and no violent struggles of nature so recently. The channel buoys were all replaced, the light ship was again at its post, and every thing exhibited a careful restoration of safety and quiet, though there were still remaining a thousand melancholy traces of the recent hurricane—the shore lined with living beings searching for lost property; and the hulls of several ships were still visible. I was permitted by the very kind commander, lieutenant Pritchard, to remain on deck; and as we passed out, he pointed to the timbers of a vessel then occasionally seen, and said, "there is all that can be discovered of an American liner, (the Brothers or Pennsylvania, I now forget which; however both were wrecked near each other,) that I saw going to pieces, and from which I was supplicated, by more than a hundred voices, in the most heart-rending tones, to render assistance, which I was compelled to pass by unregarded; for, had it been in my power to have saved them, I should not have dared to do it. By rendering them assistance, and endangering your lives, and risking your escape, would have been placing my commission, my freedom, and even my life, and thereby the support of my numerous family, in jeopardy."

He conversed freely upon the subject of Canadian troubles, of our position, and probable fate, and of his own life, circumstances, and family. Like many other English gentlemen I have since met, he commiserated our misfortunes, and hoped we might be permitted to return to our homes. "Your treason, no doubt," said he, "proceeded from mistaken virtue, and therefore it cannot be considered as disgracing or unfitting you for society or trust; though doubtless, in our opinion, as Englishmen, it is highly culpable and offensive. Yet I do not deny that our government is arbitrary, or, at least, partial; of which I am in myself a sad proof. These wounds, [exhibiting a disabled hand, and a sabre cut across the face,] "were received in her service, on the deck of Nelson's flag ship, where I fought in the capacity of a junior Lieutenant, though quite young; I have ever since been in active employment; indeed, my family would have starved without it, and I am still *no higher that a senior Lieutenant,* although I have repeatedly obtained honorable commendations, (empty sounds) for what are termed 'gallant and meritorious conduct'." I dare not repeat any more of his conversations, for fear of evil consequences to him; for our soldiers, poor and in active service, to be guilty of meddling in politics counter to the ruling powers, or censure a superior's conduct, by the laws of his service, he is disgraced while the bread of his family is taken from them. This was not the only officer of the kind, whose attachment to the service of their country I have found held only by the brittle thread of interest, and who would change the moment they had an opportunity. I have frequently been struck with astonishment, at the idea of these poor men periling their lives in the support of a government that so deeply slights and tyrannises over them, giving them pay that is barely sufficient for sustenance, while it expects them to maintain a state, or rather an appearance of gentlemanly wealth and grandeur.

I was highly gratified with the humanity of the commander, and enjoyed the fine prospect afforded by a view of the hold and rocky shores of the "land's end" of England, close to which our boat "steamed rapidly" past. We sailed very near "Plymouth harbor," where Lieutenant Pritchard's family resided; that brought fresh recollections to his mind, and gave rise to new conversation, that did honor to him as a father, husband, and friend.

Just before entering Portsmouth, by the unanimous request of my companions, I addressed to Mr. Pritchard a note expressive of our deep regard for his unvaried humanity, and the intrepid conduct he manifested during the late gale, which we begged he would receive as the only means in our power of expressing our gratitude. It was a duty we owed his merit, and would feel honored by his acceptance. He received it with evident satisfaction and pleasure, and said he would "long retain it, as a memento of more value than the applause of the rich or the powerful."

We also desired he would request the authorities, into whose hands he would place us, to permit us to occupy some room distinct from the general gangs. He promised to comply, and when we had landed he informed me that he had done so successfully.

About two P.M. of the 16th, we moored to the dock in Portsmouth, and proceeded directly to the Leviathan, a mammoth hulk lying close to an immense dock yard, where most of the numerous convicts of this station were employed. While there we were visited by several officers of the navy, whose curiosity suggested many questions connected with our cases and the Canadian grievances, which we cautiously answered, not willing to satisfy impertinence at the expense of discretion.

Sir Philip Durham, Admiral of the station, accompanied by Lieut. Pritchard, approached us, when I was named as "the man whose life had been saved by the unparalleled conduct of his wife, who had made a journey of seven hundred miles, to present, personally, her petitions to his Lordship, the Earl of Durham."

Sir Philip informed me at once, that the Earl was a brother of his, whose administration, he was highly gratified to learn, had given unusual satisfaction to the Canadian people. He spoke of his brother's elevated character as a statesman, counsellor, and liberal politician; and was sorry such baneful conduct had been exhibited by the ministry, as to cause his resignation of a government which had already exhibited some felicitous effects, and whose most prominent features had been generous humanity. He hoped the reconciliatory policy recommended by his Lordship would be critically tested, for not until then could his services be fully appreciated. Every sentiment expressed by Sir Phillip on this point, found a responsive feeling in my breast, and I too hoped his latter policy might obtain a full and proper trial; for I really anticipated much present benefit from it for the Canadas, the Upper at least.

He expressed himself heartily glad that we had manifested a desire to keep as far as possible from other prisoners, whom, generally speaking, we would always find a "set of infamous wretches, whose immorality, obscenity, and common vicious propensities, could not be held in too great abhorrence, and which must inevitably reflect disgrace upon every associate." He sincerely desired we would continue to maintain such a feeling, and show ourselves worthy the commiseration so universally exhibited.

"In this hulk," said he, "where the worst of England's criminals are confined, you would not, if you receive their own tale, find one man guilty of the slightest punishable offence." He highly commended the strenuous efforts made in London, by the united abilities of so many great minds, but he feared it might all be attributable to party purposes.

My conceptions of the wretchedness existing on board those hulks, were in no manner diminished by the description given by the Admiral, or the haggard and ludicrous appearance of the few beings, who, in the discharge of their duty, had passed us; and I began to despond at the idea of becoming a settled resident and realizing the character invariably given to those great floating prisons. The boat that came to convey us away was reported, and we went on board, after bidding adieu to the soil of England, upon which we were never again to set foot. We arrived at the York about four, rowed by a set of wretched looking convicts, and mounted its side with a deep gloom, a melancholy foreboding, a sad heaviness of heart, that I could not hope to have dispelled by the reception within its interior. We stood at last upon the quarter deck, whither our luggage soon followed. Its quantity evidently surprised the officers who stood there; and, no doubt, they already, in fancy, enjoyed the plunder of it, which they afterwards actually perpetrated.

The commander, Mr. Nicholson, in his address, told us it would be necessary to take what money, tobacco, &c, that we might have in our possession; and it would be best to surrender it, for if any was found afterwards, the crime would be a heinous one, and punished in an exemplary manner; as no traffic, or use of tobacco was permitted. After all the money was given up, (which was precious little indeed), our persons, pockets, and caps were closely "frisked" (searched), for fear some had been secreted. We were then taken to another part of the ship where the irons were all knocked off. While that was proceeding, Mr. Greetham, a barrister of Portsmouth, with his lady, arrived, and enquired for me. I found he had been appointed by J. A. Roebuck, Esq., as our resident agent; and that he had come off to receive and impart whatever instructions were necessary to open a correspondence with London; and offer all assistance he could render, consistent with the regulations of the *hulk*. This appointment of a convenient agent, exhibited, on the part of our London friends, an anxiety to serve, or, at least, a generous desire to *calm* our minds; and, indeed, it almost dispelled the doubt that I had given way to, on our removal to that place from Liverpool.

This favor was indeed extraordinary, particularly as it was extremely seldom, if ever permitted, to any who once enter those walls, where they are shut from all friendly intercourse for the term of their durance, save one visit annually, from a wife, child, or parent.

Lieutenant Pritchard came off and reported our characters, perhaps more favorably than we deserved, as follows: "They are mostly men of property, respectability, and family. Mr. Batcheldor could not have given better characters than he did to these men; and all their conduct on board my vessel warrant the highest encomiums; and, I would add, they are intelligent, *praying*, men." This great strain about character, which I found to be very common indeed among men who could not be supposed to possess any but the most heinous, I could not then see the full force of; and therefore laughed at the idea, as a mere burlesque upon the word. But since, I have frequently discovered, that every *thing* must have a character, and *that* is one great point of their system of prison discipline.

The next move was to the washing ward, where we were stripped, underwent an ablution, and a complete transformation, by the assumption of the "hulk dress," consisting of a coarse spotted guernsey frock, hemp shirt, and a pair of short knee breeches, jacket, and waistcoat, of coarse thin gray cloth. A thin pair of gray long stockings, a coarse check cotton neckerchief, a pair of low cowskin shoes, and to *cap* all a coarse stiff wool hat; every article of which was marked, remarked and marked again, with the "crow's foot" (broad arrow). When last, though not least, a large iron band of near four pounds weight, extremely rusty, was put on each right leg the following day. Thus carrying out to the fullest extent their *iron* policy. Besides the broad arrow, in a number of places the number of each, as entered on the books, was also stamped on each article of dress. The clothes we wore were all bundled together and given to the steward, whose man, (a convict,) attended to observe that no articles were retained, not so much even as a handkerchief.

Thus transformed, I am sure none of our former friends could have selected me from a number of beings so clad; in fact, I scarce knew myself, by feelings, appearance or any thing else. Yet this metamorphosis was not sufficient, for the following day our whiskers were shaved and hair sheared close to the head in such a manner, that you would have scarce known that we had ever possessed either. This was a *cruelty* for the stiff hats did not shield our heads; and the consequences were immediate violent colds and catarrhs.

The apparel of these hulks I viewed as a peculiar badge of disgrace, and the iron band as the stern token of unmitigated slavery. And it was not with much calmness, that I regarded the progress made in the gradual scale the government pursued, in their determination to assimilate us, as much as possible to the condition, character and appearance of the "world's most degraded wretches," preparatory to their immersing us into this present undistinguishable state of debasement.

I remain, dear sir,
Yours, &c. &c.

The Hulk "York"

10

Routine on the Hulk

Ashgrove, near Oatlands, V.D.L.
March, 1841.

To ——,

My Dear Sir: —

The York is the hull of an old 74, three deck man of war, built many years ago, upon which Admiral Lord Howe hoisted his flag; but proved too dull and sluggish to be brought into action, she was returned home, and condemned to an inactive life. She was immediately dismantled, and transformed to a prison ship; and was, for many years, only used however as a hospital. But for the last few years the home convict establishment having been brought into a narrower compass, she has been occupied by about 400 convicts, besides the hospital, which contains now usually nearly 125 men. She has a spacious upper deck, upon which we promenaded in as desolate a state of mind as can well be imagined, until the approach of our bed hour, when each shouldered his hammock and followed a guide, to the lower deck level with the water where we entered one, of fourteen wards, seven on each side of the narrow hall, each calculated to contain 40 men. The sides of the ship in each ward were pierced for two guns, but the apertures then were secured by iron bars, and, at night closed with dead lights.

The front, adjacent the hall, was divided from it by iron grates, but from the collateral wards by wooden partitions across the hall from those occupied, and the companion way to the chapel on the middle deck, went up from the intermediate space nearly opposite our ward; the hatch of which was off, so that we were open to the atmosphere of the chapel, the hall, and the three other wards, whose ports were all up. It was January, and the weather was exceeding cold; yet, notwithstanding all these *frigid* facts, the ten Canadians, (for Gemmel had been sent to the hospital,) were put there to sleep, with a hammock slung that only contained a straw *palleasse*, two old blankets, and one rug each. When once retired we attempted to compose ourselves to rest; but with myself and some others, it was wholly nugatory. I could, with more ease and comfort, have slept, covered up in one of our North American snow banks—cold and hunger combined, (for there we were, out of the reach of individual charity, and suffered the consequence of the ration laws I have elsewhere described,) prevented my resting. My body became perfectly chilled, and my limbs so benumbed, that, although I paced the ward for the most of the night with a quickened step, yet I could not, for my life, shake completely off what I felt was the lassitude of death. That night's frost did its work; for to this distant day I do, and, most probably, to my last hour, shall feel its painful effects upon both my feet.

In a truly forlorn condition the morning dawned upon us, and soon brought our breakfast, which consisted of a quarter of a pound of ship biscuit, and one pint of oat meal gruel called, in the prison slang, "skilly", alias, "smiggins". The biscuit I could eat; but the gruel, notwithstanding my extreme hunger, I could not endure.

Immediately after the morning meal was consumed, the ten occupied wards were emptied, and their tenants, were sent to the shore at work, raising an embankment upon the Chelsea beach, which was invariably washed away, at each succeeding high wind. We were then also unlocked, and permitted to carry our hammocks to the unsheltered upper deck, and there peragrate for the day unemployed, save by furbishing our irons which we were directed to do, and answering the questions of every petty officer of the hulk who chose to interrogate us. By and bye, I had nearly forgotten to mention, that we were not wholly alone in the ward, for a felon was sent among us to sleep for the avowed purpose of "teaching us hulk manners, and hulk rules", and for the disavowed purpose of reporting contingent circumstances; the latter might as well have been omitted, for the sequel will show that we needed no minute watching, for our murmurs and complaints were not "breathed out in secret"; but were *"published* in London at the very threshold of St. James'."

Our dinner consisted of a very little salt, a pint of 'beef tea' (i.e. the well skimmed liquid in which fresh beef had been boiled), a half pound of half boiled beef, including bone, and one pound of the coarsest, sourest, blackest, and most unpalatable bread you can possibly imagine, made of horse beans and barley, as I am informed; the crust is generally burned, and as uneatable as a brick bat, but the residue is so adhesive, that if you should roll a lump in your hand and throw it against the wall, it would there remain until torn away. The following day, instead of meat and broth, we got a half pint of sour "swipes" (ale), and a quarter of a pound of tough dry cheese, with a rind so hard, that it could not be cut through by the force of the hand; indeed, I would as soon attempt to eat CAUTCHOU. These dinners vary every third day, but the morning and evening meals are unvaried in their usual routine of nauseous oat meal.*

---

*Extract of a letter I wrote to J. Hume Esq., M.P., which was sent through the office of the Secretary of State.

In the morning I lost no time in applying for an addition to our beds, which was complied with. Therefore when the second night approached, after drinking my pint of hot gruel, I swung my hammock, retired to rest, and was awakened, by the morning gun invigorated and refreshed.

Another species, of what we termed affront, appeared in the shape of a being in the "convict garb", coming to our ward door, at retiring time, and reading the "church service", while we had to respond "amen" at the close of each prayer. We had always maintained the habit of morning and evening devotions in an extemporaneous method, and, therefore, felt this a grievance we ought not to submit to, without a trial to evade. This, with the provision, formed the subjects of a consultation among ourselves, when one of the men expressed himself very happily as follows: "I look upon the present fare, as wholly uncongenial to American constitutions: and I pray to God in the language of England's dominant church, for that government which we would have gladly driven from the American Continent, and for that Queen's welfare who had enslaved, and was starving us, was utterly inconsistent with Canadian patriotism: nay, it is treason to our cause; for it supplicates destruction to our interest. If we pray at all, let us pray for the success of the cause of truth, justice, and liberty! then if our desires are answered, it will be, for good and not for evil: and if we maintain the character we have tried to establish we will not submit without remonstrance." Bravo! sounded from every tongue, and I was instantly deputed to wait on the Commander with a request to alter the provisions, and permit us to worship God in the form we preferred. That part relative to the worship, was immediately conceded; but to alter our rations, was more than his situation was worth, for he held the tenure of his office during the good will and pleasure of the principal superintendent; however he would confer with Mr. Williams, surgeon of the hospital, who, no doubt, would, on his recommendation, put us upon hospital diet, if we would consent to the change. I of course, was agreeable to any change, provided it would only oust the "skilly" and "brown tommy".

I returned to our lodgings and "reported progress", which gave general satisfaction. The change of diet was effected, and it then consisted of one pint of rice and milk in the morning, three fourths of a pound of good white bread, one fourth of a pound of good mutton, one potatoe, and a pint of broth, for dinner; and for supper one pint of tea, well milked and sugared. This food was good but of very short allowance; yet the quality made up for quantity, and I felt myself greatly relieved from the acidity of the stomach and lassitude that the ship's diet produced. A diarrhoea had commenced that I verily believe would have terminated the existence of some of our men had not this change taken place. The third day after arrival we received per a convict servant, an order to repair to a certain ward, and have our "likeness taken". We went to the place designated, and were individually brought before the Commander, and closely interrogated by him as follows, while every reply was carefully inserted in an immense folio, by a convict clerk:

"What is your name? What is your age? What is your trade? What is your religion? Where were you arrested? Where were you tried? What was your sentence? (Ans. death—not satisfactory.) What was your commuted sentence? (Ans. transportation.) For what length of time? (do not know.) 'Put them down life'. When were you tried? When did you leave Canada? Are you married? (if married) Is your wife living? Where does she reside? Of what religion is she? Have you any children? How many males? How many females? What sex is the oldest? What sex is the youngest? What are their respective ages? Are your parents living? Where do they reside? What is their native country? What are their respective ages? What is their religion? Can they read? Can they write or keep accounts? Can you read, write or keep accounts? What is your number?"

After the answers to these questions were duly recorded each one of us, in rotation, was directed to strip naked to the waist, and up to the knee, when every spot, scar, mole, and other mark on the person—color of the hair on the head and person—color and shape of the eye and brow—shape of mouth, nose and chin, with the general appearance of the features; and, finally, the number of teeth lost; with our height, weight, and every other indication whereby our person might be identified, in the event of an attempt at escape, were particularly inserted and afterwards read over to each, and signed with his own hand.

This then completed our "likenesses"; and they were so particularly taken, that either of us could have been detected at any place, by those descriptions.

Those small tokens made of paper, in the shape of hearts, that I have before mentioned, here soon became beneficial to me and others; as I had the good fortune to exhibit some of them to an officer on board, who was so taken with the curiosity, that he begged, and carried them on shore, where Miss Strickland, (Compiler of the Queen of Scots Letters) who kept a Bazar, prized them very highly and sent off several sheets of colored paper, to have a lot made for her, with strict orders for "the maker's name and patriotic mottoes to be carefully imprinted upon them". This manouver had to be done "on the sly," but it contained several loaves of good bread. On the approach of St. Valentine's day, which is highly regarded there, the demand was greatly increased, and our pay redoubled; but these, at last, became an "old story," recourse was had to small boxes, and horsehair rings, with partial success for a time.

I mention this little circumstance as elucidatory of the ingenuity of man, when reduced to necessity; it not only furnished the occasional luxury of an additional *loaf* but, likewise, the cause of many remarks upon the industrious habits, and inventional powers of the American character, that gained us respect, and good opinion.

The officers, generally, were indeed very agreeable, and took apparently, some pleasure in conversing with us, particularly in respect to our grievances, and the condition of the Canadas; when they would occasionally draw conclusions from the information so obtained, and make contrast between what they could call "the happy state of North America, and poor *beautiful England*".

An assistant Surgeon, a young man of considerable talent and promise, (a Mr. Elliot,) one day, after passing many eulogiums upon "favored America," where he would really like to emigrate to, if it was in his power, said, "you complain of the provisions you receive here, but I can tell you there are six millions of Britains *free* subjects, who would feel themselves happy in getting one half you do; though you think it is short allowance, and coarse stuff; yes, there are thousands who annually commit crime for no other purpose than to become imprisoned in these cages of infamy, and to avoid a residence in the parish workhouse. Indeed, to an abode there, I should myself prefer transportation, and take my chance amid the congregated mass of perfidy in New South Wales."

This information was even correct; for I have been since told, by several on board that hulk, and very many here, *that, although their food* was *coarse and scanty*, and *they* were, in reality, the *slaves* of *caprice*, yet the whole was far superior to what they had usually been accustomed to—that they had never known satiety, and would not *exchange* present *bondage*, under the cat, for their former freedom!! Is there no remedy for this unhallowed condition? Could not the *great* British government devise some means to curtail this cause of so vast an amount of criminal abandonment? Indeed, it could be done, notwithstanding the late assertion of a prominent Minister, "that the distress was beyond the reach of Parliamentary enactment." The secret is, *they will not listen to a syllable on retrenchment.* A moderately less sordid policy, would relieve their paupers of one half their present misery; but such a step would reduce the aristocracy to the *contemptuous* necessity of economizing. The poor laborer would be raised too near the level of the lordling, and be no longer obliged to crouch beneath their withering scowl, nor stand at an humble distance, with hat in hand, *imploring* employment at any price, to *only* momentarily check approaching starvation. Grant the people justice, make them less miserable, less depraved, less dependent, and they will stand up more like men, to *demand* what is their due. The lordling is so engrossed by his own vicious pursuits, and the gratification of his own sordid passions—that he heeds not the cries for bread—the voice that sounds like a trumpet from the tombs of starved millions, as a warning of impending wo. Avarice closes every avenue to their hearts, and not a ray of compassion finds its way there, to soften their obduracy—power and aggrandizement are their whole aim—tyranny and misery are the effects of their success; while they who commisserate, and would remedy the prevailing evils, are either crushed beneath the foot of power, or are suffered to spend their days in vain attempts, limiting their benevolence to the wretched of their own immediate neighborhood.

What a load of wo is in store for the *"tyrants* of England"; and as assuredly as there is a just God ruling the destinies of the nations of the earth, she will receive her full weight.

But I am indulging in portraying what you were personally acquainted with years ago.

I remain, dear sir,
Yours, &c. &c.

Ashgrove, near Oatlands, V.D.L.
April, 1841.

To ——,
My Dear Sir: —
Soon after we had become a little accustomed to the circumstances of our new abode and dress, we began to think of complying with the requests of our friends in London, by giving them a brief detail of all we had endured since the first insurrectionary movements in our Province, as Mr. Greetham had, for that purpose, brought off a good supply of paper, pens, and ink. He also had brought several letters from Joseph Hume, Esq., M.P., W.H. Ashurst, Esq., Mr. Waller, and some other gentlemen, with a great number from our countrymen in New Gate. Mr. Hume particularly desired me to write for him a description of our situation, food, clothing, &c. on board the hulk, to enable him, if necessary, to apply at the proper place for an alleviation, which I did nearly the same as I have given yourself; and most probably I mentioned the circumstance of having applied to the officers on board, for a removal from the ward we inhabited, on account of the extreme cold, to another we had discovered to be vacant, that had been used as a "dead house," but then was "cleared out," another having been substituted for it, in which I had been unsuccessful, mainly through the undeserved evil opinion of the principal surgeon of the hospital, excited by the pestilential communications of the *traitor Beemer;* for the surgeon held a violent antipathy toward me from the day of my placing the letter in the office, where he must have seen and read it, on which account I believe he made us return to the ship's from Hospital diet. However, be that as it may, and whether I did relate that particular incident or not, I cannot now recollect, as I did not retain a copy of the letter; for writing was rendered extremely difficult from the cold: Yet it was apparent that something was wrong in his estimation, for my letter was closely followed by one from him, in which he indulged in unheard of virulence and vituperation against me, that produced a short note from Mr. Hume, enclosing one from the Under Secretary of State, requesting it might be returned to him with remarks.

Mr. Hume's note, the Secretary's letter, and my reply, I subjoin, to permit you to judge of the spirit manifested therein, which you can do better by a perusal of the originals, than by my conclusions.

Bryanston's Square,
13th February, 1839.

Mr. Hume begs to send the answer he has received from the Under Secretary of State, to the complaints which Mr. Wait made to Mr. Hume, of the accommodation and treatment of the Canadian prisoners. And Mr. Hume hopes their unfortunate situation will be made as comfortable as the rules, applicable to all prisoners under orders for transportation, will admit of. Mr. Hume requests the letter may be returned, with any observations Mr. Wait may think proper to make in relation thereto; but Mr. Hume hopes that no unnecessary trouble will be given to either party.

Mr. Benj'n Wait, York Hulk.

Thus ended Mr. Hume's laconic, repulsive note: yes, and thus ended his *boasted* liberal endeavors in bringing about a "restoration to our sorrowing families," or of "an alleviation" of the horrid sufferings we were then enduring. Perhaps the intimation at the close of Mr. Fox Maule's letter, had the expected effect of deterring him from his promised kindness.* However, be that as it may, we heard nothing farther from him, not even an acknowledgment of the receipt of my reply to, and the return of Mr. Maul's letter.

Home Secretary's Office,
February 10, 1839.

My Dear Sir:

I am directed by the Secretary of State, to return you the letter written and signed by the convict Wait, in behalf of his companions, purporting to give you a true account of their situation on board of the York hulk. I accompany it with some remarks I was desired to make, which, it is hoped, will convince you that his sufferings are not as great as he represents.

I have written to the officer on board the hulk, and find they occupy the ward we directed they should be placed in; it is the same from which the boys were taken a month or two ago, when they were sent to the penitentiary at Rye, on the isle of Wight; and excepting the late alterations of the weather, I do not see why it is not as habitable for its present, as for its former occupants. He complains of the two preliminary processes of cutting off the hair, and assuming prison dress.

The reason assigned for the first is, to prevent the generating of vermin, which every means must be used to guard against in a community like the hulks; and I do not anticipate its being done in an *'inhuman manner.'* The assumption of prison dress is, to afford a corresponding chance of detection, in an attempt to escape, when on shore at work.

---

*Since my return I have learned by Mrs. Wait, that Mr. Hume intimated to her, while in England, that had her husband regarded truth more in his complaints, he would not have abandoned him. *"Truth more,"* here means, *less independence*—less *bitterness* of feeling.

As to the coldness of the ward they inhabit, I am told that a hanging stove was allowed them during the greatest severity of the weather.

And the provisions supplied them, is the same in quantity and quality, furnished to thousands of prisoners before them, by the government, without complaint; and several years experience, and the united opinions of various physicians, have taught us that it is perfectly wholesome, and sufficient for the actual necessities of any man, notwithstanding the assertion of the convict Wait, and his fellow convicts, to the contrary.

There were no orders issued from this office, for a difference of treatment from the *other* felons, except that, by their own request, they were to be kept separate from them, and not to be sent out to work. Wait may be assured, that his letters, when written with such an independant spirit, and in such a tone of presumption, cannot pass unheeded.

When you have perused this letter, please return it, with whatever pertinent remarks may occur to you. And I am directed to say, you will do well to abstain from receiving the convict Wait's complaints of ill treatment, when in the custody of the officers of our government, for he is a cunning, designing fellow, and his associate convicts are his dupes.

> I am, Sir, your obd't
> Humble serv't,
> Fox Maule,
> Under Secretary of State.

Joseph Hume, Esq., M.P.

The contents of the foregoing letter were astounding indeed. The frequent repetition of "convict Wait," and the "other felons," sounded in my brain for a long while. I could not imagine what had been the Secretary's motives for descending to such low, abusive language, or what ends, save traduction, he had to answer by it. However, I deemed it giving me a license to reply in an equally disrespectful style. It accounted at once for the *hauteur* with which the surgeon had already treated me, and the coldness of Mr. Humes' laconic note. My reply was as follows:

> York Hulk,
> February 15, 1839.

My Dear Sir:

Your *laconic* note of the 13th inst. was handed me by Mr. Greetham, and which was accompanied by Mr. Fox Maule's singularly sophistical letter; the perusal of it has truly given me no little surprise.

I am indeed grieved to discover the Secretary capable of such low, scurrilous expressions, and assertions so positively false; and which, I have reason to believe, he knew to be so. For, on receiving your letter, I went with it directly to the commander, whom I supposed to be the "officer on board" he means, and from whom he ought to have received his information. But he is equally surprised with myself, and cannot surmise what "officer on board" could have originated such falsehoods. I cannot give him, (Mr. Maule,) credit for being even ordinarily 'cunning', for mark his position; when speaking of the ward we occupy, he says, 'it is the same from which the boys were taken a *month* or *two* ago, when sent to the penitentiary, ** and *excepting* the *late alterations* of the weather, I do not see why it is not as habitable for its present as its former occupants.

Here allow me to remark, that 'a month or two ago,' 'the late alterations of the weather' had not taken place; that it was then warm, but now it is *cold;* and we all know that a room naturally cold from its locality, is much more 'habitable' in the fine weather of summer, or autumn, than during the cold, frosty months of winter. It is true, 'the ward is the same from which the boys, (or a part of them,) were taken,' not *'a month* or *two,'* but *three months ago.* But even suppose it had been during last week that they were removed, I would appeal to himself, or any other person equally inimical to humanity, to say, whether the atmosphere of any space, when occupied by eighty persons, would not be heightened far above what it is possible to be, when inhabited by only nine? For not only the air of the four different wards in which the eighty boys were lodged, but likewise of a chapel, calculated to accommodate five or six hundred persons, is open to us nine Canadians.

And further, his assertion about the 'hanging stove,' is an utter fabrication; as no stove, of any kind, ever made its appearance in or near our ward, during our occupancy.

As to the 'preliminary processes of cutting off the hair, and assuming prison dress,' I have only to reassure you, the former *was inhumanly done;* and, when combined with the scantiness of our wardrobe and the frigidness of our lodgings, have placed us in circumstances very nearly approaching death. And I am quite sure that our security did not render it an imperative necessity to invest our persons with the habiliments of the hulk, and our legs with the iron bands of slavery, 'as a correspodning chance for detection, in an attempt to escape when on shore at work,' for we are never permitted to leave the ship's sides; and he says their orders were against putting us at work.

In regard to what is said about the wholesomeness of the diet, I can aver that six of the nine are now severely suffering by diarrhoea, purely the effect of the sour bread we are now forced to use, as we have again been put on the ship's diet. I dare say those gentlemen and surgeons who have pronounced this food good, wholesome, and sufficient, have never tried it themselves; and have, perhaps never seen it; and there is very good reason for no complaint being made by any english convict, for the *'cat'* is the sure consequence of murmur, (called insolence.)

But for my part, I protest, that unless some salutory change is soon effected, I fully expect my lifeless body will be spirited away through one of the port holes of this ship, as an article of traffic with some London quack, whose dirty laboratory my whitened bones may grace, beside others who have gone the same road, after having taught some half-dozen students the art of dissection and anatomy.

I do most sincerely hope my letters may 'not pass unheeded', (as he is pleased to say,) but that they will have the effect desired, by causing an alleviation of some circumstances attending our residence here, or, at least, of bringing about an inquiry, which is very much required.

What designs Mr. Maule has to answer by insulting helpless prisoners in his power, by applying to us the ignominious epithets of 'convicts and felons,' are, of course, best known to himself; and I have only to say, that it indicates, in my estimation, a mind of inferior intelligence, and cowardly principles.

I certainly fancied I had good authority for saying, 'I presumed orders had been given for a treatment different from what was received by the felons on board; and, in fact, there is actually more difference existing, than I really relish; for they receive each two loaves of white bread per week, whereas the state prisoners obtain none. From the surgeon, Mr. Williams, we have repeatedly received abusive language, that savors more of the Billingsgate creature, then the gentleman; and I ardently hope a removal from his proximity will soon be affected, though it be into perpetual slavery.

In a former letter I particularly described our condition; not one syllable of which, although repugnant to the authorities, am I willing to retract.

And now, in reply to your own note, I would merely say, that I am heartily sorry for having given as much trouble, necessary or unnecessary, as I have already done, to either party; and shall, for the future, endeavor, as much as possible, to abstain from it.

I would here beg to tender, not only my own, but all my countrymen's gratitude, for the kindness and generosity with which you seemed to have been actuated in espousing our causes, while, my dear sir, not only for myself, but in behalf of suffering humanity, I subscribe myself

Yours truly,
Benjamin Wait.

Joseph Hume, Esq. M.P., London

Of these letters I retained copies; and a few days after had an opportunity of exhibiting them to Mr. Capper, the principal superintendent, who had come to the hulks on a visit of enquiry, and remained for a week. He arrived on Saturday, and on Sunday he sent for me, while we were in the chapel listening to the murder of the story of Joseph, by an imbecile old priest, who occupied five Sabbaths in its relation. I had not been informed of the arrival of Mr. Capper, and consequently did not know for what purpose I was called from that *interesting* service, by the *convict-dressed servant*, who had merely announced that "Wait was wanted". I followed, and was ushered into a finely fitted up apartment, where I observed a large elderly *man*, seated at a table apparently deeply engaged in the perusal and checking of accounts. The convict servant, (All the officers belonging to any of those establishments have each one or more servants selected from among the convicts, who do nothing but attend their master's bidding), led me to the middle of the room, and touching his hat, said, "this is Wait, sir," then retired, without having attracted the slightest attention from the man of accounts.

I stood for some minutes, until I became exhausted, when I walked to the window, endeavouring to attract notice; but, without looking up, he said, "Wait, sit down, and I will talk to you presently;" then continued his employment. I sat down, happy in the privilege, and remained some half hour or more, before the ominous silence was again broken. I mention this incident, as it is what I conceive to be a pretty fair specimen of the general manners of English business men, which they practice more for the purpose of being thought eccentric, than through any engrossed attention; for I have been introduced to perhaps a score of men in the same manner since, who have invariably conducted as though one rule governed all, while in some cases not the slightest occasion could be discovered for such abstractedness.

When Mr. Capper had apparently come to the conclusion that it was necessary to make himself known, he surprised me by saying, "well, Wait, what did you want to say to me?" I replied, that I had not intimated to any person a desire to speak with him, in fact, did not know him whom I had the honor of addressing. "Oh, yes! yes, I wanted to talk with you; I believe you are one of the men sent from Upper Canada for riot." I answered, that I had been transported for political offences, and would be glad to know the gentleman who had been kind enough to desire to speak to me. "Oh, I am the principal superintendent of the hulks, Mr. Capper, and I did not know but you had some complaints to make concerning your treatment by the officers." I told him I had no complaint to make against any officer save the Surgeon, who had not only treated me shamefully, but had likewise made some misrepresentations at the Secretary's office, which I desired he would inquire into and rectify. I also requested him to inform me what had been done with *fourteen* letters, that we had written and sent through his office, for America; and which were to have been put into the hands of our agents in London, who had been informed such letters were to come for them, to forward, some weeks since; which, however, had not been received by them. He replied, that he had delivered them, but two hours before leaving London. I desired permission to step to the ward and bring the letters that had passed, between the Secretary, Mr. Hume and myself. These he perused, and promised to enquire into the facts; but, says he, Mr. Williams says you have insulted him; yet I conceive that it is only your American manners he kicks at; and of course, you will, for the future, be less blunt in addressing him. Although you may have written nothing but what is positively true, yet it would have been better for you to have been silent, or, at least, not to have addressed Hume; for all he desires is to obtain something to use in bolstering up his decaying reputation. Per haps it would be better for you to *cut* his acquaintance now; for I can assure you, that when he has got all he can that may answer his ends, he will abandon you to shift for yourself, the worse for his interference. The secretary has been drawn into an error by somebody, and I will set him right; I will come to your ward tomorrow, *when* I want you all in."

On the following day he came, attended by Mr. Nicholson, Mr. Williams, and others; and the scene that took place I cannot omit, though I fear you will deem it too egotistical or frivolous; yet it goes to prove a particular trait of English character, that I am very desirous of holding up to scorn.

After we had been mustered in single file, Mr. Capper examined the ward, and questioned each one closely, as to how they fared, were treated &c. In our answers he found no faltering or equivocation. He also enquired how the mistake had occurred relative to the stove? I told him I thought Mr. Williams could best explain that, as he had originated it, who replied, that he had ordered one, but soon after, thinking we might burn up the ship, he had countermanded it. "Ah, indeed!" said Mr. C., "you then did give Wait occasion for charging you with known falsehood; and I discover too, that he has had reason for his complaints of cold, which would be readily obviated, by hanging canvass along the grating; and I wish it attended to immediately." This suggestion was complied with, but not until the eleventh hour; for two days afterwards, a fresh supply of convicts from London, filled the opposite and adjacent wards, so that we were freed from cold; but on the other hand, were confused, and kept in excitement, by the continual swearing, fighting, and clamor, of our neighbors; yet it gave us a fair opportunity of learning the character, and remarking the conduct of the wretches who inhabit these hot beds of iniquity. But to close the interview, Mr. Williams desired to learn whether the letters of complaint were written at the request of my companions, or at my own instance; "an individual inquiry would be more satisfactory, I thought, as all were present, and I was sure they would answer without fear." "Yes," said Mr. W. "if their audacity is equal to yours, I know, already, what they will say." "I dare say you do," I replied, "but conscious rectitude and *truth* needs not the aid of impudence or scurrility." Turning to Mr. C. he said, "did you ever hear such insolence from a convict;" then ordered me from the ward, that the men need not be "overawed" by my presence, or taught "effrontery," by my example. The evidence went to corroborate my statements fully. It was, then, "no more than (he) expected; but there was that honest Beemer, who would not endorse (my) doings; for he had already exposed our characters, in their true colors." "Indeed, I was glad to hear he had done it truly, but was fearful from late discoveries, that truth would be sadly desecrated, by being associated with his, and certain other names; yet I felt as fearless of the *'expose'* threatened, as I did of the windy, ungallant conduct, I sometimes unnecessarily witnessed." Mr. C. soon terminated these retorts, and left us to our own private musings and consultations, which resulted in a short note to Mr. Hume, signed by all but Beemer, corroborative of what I had written.

A day or two subsequent, the following document was signed and sent to the Secretary's office.

To the Right Honorable Lord John Russell,
Secretary of State for the Home Department:

My Lord:
We have to request your Lordship will favor us with an explanation, why, *we*, being STATE PRISONERS, are confined in a *felon* prison, and treated and dressed as

felons. We know of no precedent for such treatment, and consequently feel surprised to find ourselves thus circumstanced by the British government, whose boast has always been, a liberality to *prisoners of state,* and therefore enter our solemn protest against it.

> We have the honor to be your Lordship's
> ob't serv'ts
> Benjamin Wait,
> Sam'l Chandler
> Alex'r McLeod
> John Vernon
> John J. McNulty
> James Waggoner
> Norman Mallary
> Geo. B. Cooley
> Garret Van Camp

(James Gemmel being in the hospital, was not applied to for his signature.)

We were induced to hazard the foregoing protest, by the discovery, through the Under Secretary's letter, of the rancorous feeling existing toward us in the hearts of men in high office. Not that Mr. Moule was, *of himself,* a man of much importance; but sentiments written by him in a public capacity, must have emanated from his superior in office; indeed, he intimated as much, and we therefore held Lord John accountable for the conduct of his immediate servant. And, although our friends in New-Gate might be successful, yet our cases were hopeless, and could not be made worse.

We felt assured of harsh measures; for we knew that when the ministers were once so egregiously offended, they would scarcely stop short of some excessive stretch of power; for in the case of prison discipline, they have absolute control. There is no censuring power—no "public opinion" to govern in that. We saw the die was cast, and the resulting disadvantageous, therefore, determined to combat every irregularity, and submit to no onerous proceeding, without exhibiting, at least, a *spirit* of firm resistance. I dare say this spirit conduced largely toward producing our immediate removal into transportation; for the government knew full well, that, in a colony so distant, and under arbitrary administration, all complaint would be futile—*nay,* would be considered insolence, and punished rigorously.

Many letters passed between ourselves and solicitors, as well as fellow country-men in New-Gate; but my correspondence is already too much extended, and I must omit all, or, at least, extract *very briefly;* for I have much still to relate. Mr. Greetham very frequently came off, not only to see and bring us letters, but also as Coroner, to hold inquests on the bodies of all who died on board; which, however, I did not know was the case, until I one day observed a dozen rough looking boatmen come to the hulk, followed by him, and proceed to the hospital, where they remained perhaps five minutes, when they left the ship as they came, each in his own boat. Mr. G. having some letters to deliver to me, gave an opportunity for inquiring what the visit of those men meant? when I was informed that they had constituted a coroner's jury, which he was frequently under the necessity of calling, as the government orders an inquest to be held upon the bodies of all persons who die in any of its prisons or charity institutions, which operates as a sort of quietus upon the minds of the people, who might otherwise clamor about "foul play." But, then, if I should guess from the appearance of these men, they seldom, if ever, give you the trouble of enquiry, and never elicit mal-practice. In fact, they did not spend time enough on board to more than be empannelled and say, "died by a visitation of God;" and that verdict must have been dictated, for they looked too ignorant to originate such a conception. "It is indeed very true, that they never give me any trouble in explanations, for they are generally men who require all their time for the support of a family; and, therefore, the less delay the better." I was told that the coroner obtaine two pounds for each verdict, and sat upon some one and a half hundred cases yearly, without once elucidating the slightest irregularity. The pay assists in enriching one individual, while it impoverishes many, without the most trifling beneficial results!

The letters brought off were from Mr. Ashurst, Messrs. Wixon, Millar, and Parker. Mr. A. says:

The cases of the twelve prisoners here, (London,) have been very fully argued in the court of Exchequer, and, on Tuesday last, adjourned till next term. The consequence of this will be, that the twelve in London will remain here, and YOU AND YOUR COMPANIONS WILL NOT BE SENT OUT OF THE COUNTRY.

I shall try and have you brought to London, but fear there is but slight hopes of that. Nevertheless, continue your communications, for I want full materials, and address them to me as your attorney.

It is said you petitioned for pardon, and consented to the conditions of your pardon. I wish your attention to that point particularly.

Mr. Wixon details the course pursued in bringing their cases into court, and finally the adjournment, when he says:

If we are eventually unsuccessful, we will yet have gained one great point, which will convince the world that we have been unjustly dealt with; and obtain the sympathy of the good in every country on the face of the globe.

I have this day seen one of your letters, which is to be published in the 'True Sun, a paper warmly enlisted in our interests ...

By the bye, I have exposed Capt. Morton, and the Capt. Ross voyage in good style, and if he is not satisfied with that he can have more yet; so I think after all, my way of duelling is better than yours....

There is warm work in Canada about these days. Hanging and shooting is the order of the day there, but we are snugly out of harm's way here.

I learned in court, that my sentence is *fourteen years after arrival in V.D.L.*—Mr. Watson's is 'life,' and the others are yet as ignorant as ever of what time they *are ordered, (not sentenced)* for. ....

This Mr. Wixon had but one leg, was a Baptist clergyman, and whose only crime was, having acted as assistant editor of the "Correspondent and Advocate," during the absence of Mr. McKenzie, the proprietor, in England, as an agent for the people, some years prior to the insurrection.

It would indeed appear, that Arthur was rather in a strait for subjects of cruelty, when he was ordered for transportation; but that is not the greatest curiosity in his case. His time of durance would not commence until arrival in the penal Island; and he might be detained on the way an equal length of time, while age and infirmity were fast hastening him to the grave.

L.W. Miller, the gallant young American of whom you have heard so much, concludes his letter with some just structures upon the British government, by saying;

We have been in a continued excitement, owing to the *'glorious uncertainty of the law.'* ...What the result of this affair will be, no one can tell; I guess, however, It will have a tendency to open the eyes of Britons, and put a stop to their boasting of the superiority of English laws and institutions over those of other nations, inasmuch as that *'excellent safeguard of the liberty of the subject,* the *habeas corpus act'* so long lauded to the skies, has been completely shown up at last, and proved a mere *phantom—a 'will o' the wisp.'* ....Yet I flatter myself, notwithstanding the decision of the Queen's Bench Judges against us, that our cases are not quite as bad as they appear, &c. &c.

Poor fellow! He felt quite sanguine in the hope of a happy result, to the enquiry, but was disappointed, for his case, with John Grant's, being similar to ours, produced the same end—we being sent away previous to the termination of the instituted investigation, the Ministry would not hazard the imputation of partiality, by liberating him at the same time with Wixon, Parker, and their party. They, therefore, (Miller and Grant,) with Beemer, (the traitor,) and Gemmel, (whom we had left sick in the York hospital,) arrived at Hobarttown in January, of 1840, and were sent on the roads at work, in horrid destitution and want.

In addition to these letters, we received occasional numbers of the "Weekly True Sun," which contained all the arguments made in the cases of our friends, a perusal of which not only led us, but every unprejudiced mind, to anticipate a release.

An officer of the hulk handing me a paper in which the arguments were published, said, "well, Wait, that paper contains joyful intelligence for you. Your countrymen in New-Gate, although not yet acquitted, will be very soon—for the arguments against the *legality* of transportation from Upper Canada, are so conclusive, that, if the Queen is not too d-bly afraid of you, she will be glad to send you all home again, and think herself thus well rid of Arthur's blunders." But these hopes and opinions were formed on the presumptive evidence of England's doing justice; and, consequently were illusory—for *we* did not remain to learn the conclusion—but were sent hastily away.

I must here conclude this long letter, and my narrative of events while in England, with the exception of a few hulk anecdotes, which I will briefly relate in my next.

                              I remain, dear sir,
                              Yours, &c. &c.

11

ABOARD THE HULK AND A FLOGGING

Ashgrove, near Oatlands, V.D.L.
May, 1841

To ——,

My Dear Sir: —

I will now merely relate a few incidents that came under my notice before embarking for this place. I have before hinted that Beemer was the traitor to whom we owed our want of success in a certain *attempt* at sea. The discovery was effected in the following manner: we had received the form of a petition from Mr. Ashurst, desiring the government to place in his hands all letters or recommendations directed to any of us, that might arrive in England, and we were requested to sign and return it. Beemer refused, which, with his conduct in writing in another ward distinct from ours under the eye of the Surgeon, as well as some other appearances, made us suspect his faithlessness rather more strongly than before. The consequence was, a close and systematic investigation among ourselves in his presence, when one complete chain of treachery and false conduct was discovered, unbroken since our embarkation at Niagara. The first evidence was given by G. Van Camp a poor, innocent, simple, quiet Dutchman, who was Beemer's chain companion on our passage from Quebec; and this was followed up by a forcible seizure of his port-folio which contained a petition to Lord John Russell, tracing his own steps throughout the whole course, and claiming *freedom* as a boon of his *fratricidal* conduct. In the petition, he also presumed upon the commendations of Dr. Williams and Capt. Morton; but this did not end his communication, for he likewise attempted to brand our characters with infamy, by charges of a dishonorable nature, which could, in reality, attach to none but himself.

This discovery put us on the *qui vive;* and by a little inducement, we obtained a perusal of all his correspondence, from the fellow he employed to write for him, as he was very illiterate, only able to write, yet not to compose or spell—thus being enabled to counteract all his malice through the aid of our countrymen in London.

Elucidative of the utter failure, through the inefficiency of the British penal code, in the attempts to humanize hardened villains by promiscuously congregating them in these hulks, I have a large collection of anecdotes, but I cannot copy them now—for I want to devote this letter to other descriptions—suffice it therefore to say, that I will guarantee, if a man is set there for two years, though naturally circumspect in his conduct, that he goes out a polished villain, a *graduate* from the college of crime. The majority of the residents are between the ages of eighteen and thirty, though some are young as twelve; and a few thin toothless, grey headed, wretched looking fellows, numbering at least sixty *extended winters,* are seen hobbling about the decks the whole day, submitting calmly to the insults and gibes of the officers and younger felons, as if it was their "meat and their drink".

The most surprising sight and condemnatory of British institutions, that I witnessed, was the arrival, at the hulk, on their way to the Penetentiary on the Isle of Wight, of fifty boys under ten—an age in which it can scarcely be imagined they were capable of committing offences worthy the sentence of transportation, but it was so—for they were all condemned for seven, ten, or fourteen years to V.D.L. One little sprightly fellow, who said his age was seven years and five months, I took a fancy to enquire of concerning his history—he suprised me by saying he had been tried for picking a gentleman's pocket of a purse containing nine guineas and thirteen shillings with a few *"haporths"*. But how in the name of common sense could you pick a *man's* pocket? Why you could scarce reach his waist. But, "oh I didn't frisk his pocket—I was in a stall where *a* sells rings—he come'd in, and pick'd out one that suited him—just as he was going to pay for it, the shopman called him over to t'other end of the room, and I whip't up his purse and run'd away with it; I meets my sister close by the door, and slips it into her apron, and she goes right home and guv it to mother but I run on till a 'trap' nabbed me because I was running—the gentleman come up and said I stole his *purse,* they frisked me and couldn't find it; but he swore I took it; so I got lagg'd for seven years. Mother keeps the money, tho', and I'm sorry I couldn't have the bit o' plum puddin she promised me, if I would get her a good *swag* that day." Have you done any thing before? "Oh yes, I picked up a handkerchief and two *testers* the day before and mother give me a penny bunn and haporth of *yale.*" Have you got any brothers? "Yes, George was transported with father to V.D.L., for *taking* plate from the Duke's house; and I've got two sisters, one in the house of correction, and one at home, who goes every day for mother's *quarteen* of rum and pot of *yale.*" What! a father and brother in V.D.L., a sister in the house of correction, and you on the way to a penetentiary? "no, no; I'm transported." A Dr. Elliott, standing by, explained "that it was customary to pass the sentence of transportation, and then leave it optional with the ministry to retain them at the Penetentiaries or send them on; and with boys, the latter is frequently done, when there remains but a few months of their sentence unexpired." This I have found, is the case with men also, two of whom came in the same ship with me, whose sentence expired in six months after arrival here.

My next inquiry was of the one I took to be the oldest; he was nine years and some months, and was "lagged innocently for ten years to the '*Bay*'." He had no parents. "I was bound, by the parish warden, to a brush maker, who beat me so unmercifully that I couldn't stay—so run'd away and come up to London, where I lay in a cellar, on straw, for four nights; and could get nothing to eat all the time. One day I was so hungry I thought I should starve; so I begged of some gentlemen, who swore at me, and threatened to send me to the work house. I asked some ladies, but they wouldn't give me any thing; so I lay down on the steps of a house, and a police man took me to a station house. I cried, and told him I was hungry; but he wouldn't give me any thing to eat until the next day, when I was taken to the inspectors. I told them where I came from, and who my master was and how he had beat me. They sent for him, and scolded him—then sent me back with him. He used me harder than ever, but gave me a new pair of trowsers. I soon went away again, but he followed me, and swore I stole his trowsers; so I got ten years '*lagging*' to do, for it." I asked him if he would go back, providing they would allow it, and put up with his master's beatings? His answer was, that he would be better off, and would rather be flogged every day, than go back to his old master.

These boys had been away scarcely a week before the latter mentioned, and some others, were sent back to the hulk as irreclaimable characters. The lads said it was for breaking open the cellar and taking some potatoes to roast, and some of the boys "*come it*" on them.

The foregoing is a scene Americans will hardly believe; nevertheless it is true, and not of rare occurrence either. These little villains have mostly been tutored by their parents, and trained to theft and crime; and between five and eight hundred of them are annually sent out to this island, as servant boys and butlers to the settlers.

Among the arrivals from London, (for when we were on the hulk it was the season for replenishing,) was a band of wretched looking fellows, clad in rags, (having sold all their better clothing to our country-men in New-Gate,) and excessively filthy, with beard apparently a month old—clearly exhibiting the imperative necessity of the "two preliminary processes of cutting off the hair and assuming prison dress," in that case at least.

They were loaded with galling irons and seemed to be weighed down with hunger and fatigue. I stood near the quarter deck and saw them searched. Some had tobacco and money stowed away in their rags, others in their mouths and elsewhere; but few escaped with a shilling left, as the examiners were adepts in the search, and what was not willingly given up, was a legal prey to the finder. There were twenty-seven of them convicted at the last assize in London, for street robbery, and house breaking; and were all sent on the same ship with us, to this place; after turning in, they could be heard until very late, entertaining their hammock neighbors with tales of their vagrant exploits, while to question them about their offences, you would imagine they were suffering wrongfully, forcibly reminding one of an Irish convict, who wished to elicit the sympathy of a passer by for a "pipe of tobacco or a *shilling.*" "But pray," says the accosted, "what brought you here?" "Oh," answers pat with a menial touch of the hat, "it was for *staleing* a halter, that I got fourteen years." "What a hardship!" repeats the gentleman, "here's a half crown for you." "But stop," returns pat, while *fobbing the shiner*, "I've not tould ye that a horse was at the end on't."

The hulk rules are very strict—the cat was the sure consequence of money or tobacco being found in the possession of a prisoner and solitary confinement on bread and water, for the slightest traffic—yet money and tobacco were among them—but they commanded an extraordinary high value, and were great commodities for traffic; for instance, a penny could buy a man's daily allowance of "brown tommy" and meat; or a "ha'penny" his cheese and "swipes". When the "shore laborers" were passing down the ship's sides, an officer, usually the first mate, stood at the gangway to "frisk" them, to prevent their carrying any thing on shore belonging to the ship; and the same precaution was taken when coming on board, that no tobacco, or other illicit articles, might be brought off. An Hiberian, who had a home, in an affray, received a blow on the head, for friendship's sake, that cracked his skull affecting his brain, and occasioning fits of hallucination, was bringing in his mouth, a small portion of the forbidden weed. Unfortunately the officer, (Mitchard,) either having some intimation of it, or deep grudge against him, unceremoniously thrust his fingers into Pat's mouth, who, as unformally compressed them rather tightly. The mate struck the man in the face; the blow was returned, when the poor Irishman was brought to the deck by some bystanders. He was taken immediately to the quarter deck, where he received the sentence of "thirty-six on the bare back, in sight of all hands, on the following morning at eight A.M." Consequently, at the hour appointed, the men were all mustered on deck, where the poor fellow was lashed to the mizzen mast, naked to the waist, prepared to receive the stripes from the boatswain, who stood awaiting orders to begin, with his cat in hand: which was, in this case, a stick of about eighteen inches long, with nine throngs, three feet long, twisted as hard as wire, and the thickness of a man's small finger. The surgeon, whose duty it is to witness these scenes, was there and the commandant also, who offered the culprit an abatement of one half the sentence, if he humbly beg the pardon of the offended dignitary, who was likewise present. But throwing a wild gaze upon him, he looked the rage of a thousand demons, and told them to do their worst, and he would "yet have the hearts blood of the brute," who really was a concatenation of all that was evil. This answer was considered insolence, and the boatswain was ordered to lay it on without forbearance. He ran his fingers carefully down the cat, separating the throngs, so as to give each a chance to do its duty; then whirling the whip about his head, and rising, with a spring forward, gave the first blow, that, in reality, ought to have counted nine. It told a horrible tale upon the back of the poor fellow, whose skin was cut through in a dozen places; while he, without writhing, calmly cast his eyes about, as if to ask, "do I bear it well?" But a painful thrill ran through the crowd, and a sudden catching of the breath, or sigh, that was perfectly audible. The blows were repeated at intervals of forty seconds, with the same result, until two dozen were received; when the same proposal of abatement of the remainder was made with the same effect. The flagellation went on; and when completed, the poor man's back was literally beat into a jelly. He was loosened and let down a wild maniac, and the first movement was a rush at the wretch who was the cause of such inhuman severity; but, unfortunately, he was "brought up" by some of the guards standing by. The common punishment for petty offences, is confinement, on bread and water, in a solitary "black hole," where the person never sees the light within his durance, which sometimes extends to seven, and even ten days.

Trafficing is strictly forbidden, yet often winked at; as, for instance, a blind man was allowed four gallons per day of the oatmeal, which he exchanged for the white bread of the poor, half starved laborers. He also collected all the bones of the messes, pounded them fine and boiled them—in that manner extracting considerable fat, which he sold for butter—known as the "blind Jimmy's Butter." Either, *if reported*, would have gained him a few days solitary; yet the "skilly" was allowed him, and it was well known he could not consume it himself.

It was a standing rule to muster the men each Sabbath, with one bare leg, to observe their cleanliness, when their shoes must be greased, or solitary was the consequence. Now, strange to say, no provision was made for oil, and there was no possible means of obtaining but by stealing it from the lamps, two of which remained in each ward; further, should a man be detected in such theft, he would be subjected to two dozen stripes on the bare back; and to exhibit the fallacy of such rules a man is liable to a charge for insolence. Thus, then, he is placed between the horns of a dilemma, one of which seldom fails goring him; and he generally prefers the risk of theft, in which he is the least liable to be detected. In our cases, these rules were not enforced, "for," as observed by the commandant, "the Americans are men of unimpeachable moral characters—perfectly quiet and orderly —but they *will not be coerced* into compliance with any rules they consider unreasonable. They never presume upon any privileges, but when they want such, they send Wait to ask. They have thus obtained various favors that I could not have granted to other men; for instance, the use of the carpenter's shop, where it is a pleasure to observe to what extent their ingenuity and industry continue, in the manufacture of such trifles as are in their power. And at night, before they retire to their beds, I have frequently been delighted to listen to their devotions; yet they will not use our church service, and it would be ungenerous to require it; for I think them devout and pious, and know them praying men."

These remarks in favor of our character, were not the only temporal advantages received from our devotional exercises, for they, in a manner, operated also, as a beneficial check upon the conduct of some two or three of our number, who were rather vulgarly inclined. And in a spiritual sense, the good results were incalculable upon, our minds, our hearts, and our feelings. Reading and praying, enabled us to look above for consolation, in the hour of suffering and sorrow; and to give place to that hope which would not only keep us from despondency, but lead us to feel that "all things would work together for good"—that God, in his all wise providence, would give us strength according to our need, and ultimately return us to our homes and to our families. I can assure you that we have been enabled to endure every calamity and evil that has since befallen us, without much murmur or complaint, while my hope in a return to home and to freedom, is now more brilliant than ever—rendered so by a letter I have quite recently received from the still active participator in my afflictions. She has returned to Canada, and already had an interview with the Governor General, who seems favorably inclined. But more of these things anon, and I here close for the present.

> I remain, dear sir,
> Yours, &c. &c.

12

Voyage to Van Dieman's Land

Ashgrove, near Oatlands, V.D.L.
July, 1841.

To ——,
My Dear Sir: —
About the 10th March, a ship, ostensibly known as the "Bay Ship", cast anchor at Spithead; and orders came off for 140 men to be selected from the residents of the two hulks, (Leviathan and York), at Portsmouth, to make up the cargo for Van Dieman's land, already consisting of 100 men from the prison ships at Woolwich. The list for the York was some two days completing; during which time not a whisper was heard designating those who were to go; not a name was divulged. I felt a slight presentiment that our names might be added, and consequently wrote my opinions to our friends in London, desiring them to make preparations for the event, if they proved prophetic. Meeting Mr. Nicholson on the deck, I enquired if it was the intention of the government to send the American prisoners by that ship; but he replied that he was not at liberty to give satisfaction on that point; yet he had no doubt but we would have timely notice of any intended removal. Thus, then, my suspicions on that head, were allayed, and we continued our writing preparatory to the expected investigation.

On the morning of the 12th March, before we were dressed several officers were engaged in the selection and separation of those to go, from those to remain; and as they came out of the ward adjoining ours, were asked if they had any orders for us; the reply was *"no"*. This monosyllable created a laugh among us, for one of our number, (Mr. Waggoner) had said, as soon as he awaked, that "we should be sent on board the bay ship to-day, and no mistake;" yet he still persisted, and would stake his life upon the correctness of his impressions. About eight the turnkey came and unlocked the door, when we, as usual, were prepared, with hammock on shoulders, to sally forth and deposit them on the upper deck. But "stop," says the guard, "I want to muster your hammocks and bedding." This was the first move or expression that was, in the slightest degree, indicative of their intention toward us. As soon as the muster was completed, he said, "now my fine fellows, I have to inform you, that you have but five minutes to join the other prisoners in the chapel destined for V.D.L."

Those still in the ward, were McLeod, Wait, Chandler, Waggoner, McNulty, Vernon, Mallary, Cooly, and Van Camp, ordered for embarkation; Gemmel had been in the hospital since arrival; and the night previous to this, the surgeon had ordered Beemer there also; and the day we took our passage, he was under the operation of an emetic. We all knew why his retention was effected, but it eventually, by his own folly, proved of no avail. Miller, Grant and Reynolds, the others, were in London, so that our number was dwindled down to nine.

Although I should have preferred transportation, to a long continuance in that prison, yet the information of so sudden a removal, fell like an electric shock upon me, as it was utterly unexpected, after so many repeated assurances, from various individuals in office and elsewhere. I therefore begged time to write our agent, but was refused. What trifles we could hastily collect, of our small stock in the ward, were carried with us, most particularly my portfolio, containing all our correspondence in England, and the notes I had made there. This has since been my inseparable companion, and I design conveying it to America, if I am ever so happy as to return myself.

On arriving at the place of rendezvous, we found eighty or more, all invested with double irons (Two rings or *bazzles,* for the leg, with a chain between them about two feet in length, and weighing about eight pounds.) and the habiliments of the "Bay ship", the same as the *hulk* dress, saving a want of the guernsey, and the exchange of the hat for a striped woollen cap. There were prepared for out ablution, several tubs of water; and several shaving automatons were placed in requisition for clearing both head and face.

These preparations were scarcely completed before I was called to the quarter deck, where I found the commander and his *mate,* Mitchard, engaged in overhauling our baggage. I was ordered to select what belonged to myself, and then directed to open my trunk, from which Mitchard threw out every article, and then said, I might retain the trunk, but the other things, (clothes and books,) were forfeited to the government. I begged the favor of retaining a few trifling keepsakes, but all I could get was a brush, three religious books, and a wooden spoon. All my companions were treated in the same manner, and filched of everything they possessed. I accused them of robbery; for even by their own *ministerial* reasoning, we could be regarded only as being *in transitu,* and consequently, had been merely lodged temporarily in their custody, awaiting an opportunity for transportation—therefore, whatever the *transporting authorities* chose to permit us to carry from home, they had no right to rob us of in a foreign land—no more than the governor of Cape town, where we might run in for refreshment, would possess over what we might carry thence with us. All the reply they made, was, that, they knew what they were doing, and would hear nothing from me.

We were, with the other prisoners, mustered on deck, with the left leg and foot bare, (the right having the irons on,) for the purpose of inspection, by the surgeon connected with the transport ship. All were pronounced "hale and fit for the passage," until they came to me, when, from my debilitated appearance, the surgeons were induced to question me as to whether I felt able to undergo the fatigue of so long a voyage, or not? I replied that I was more fit to go than remain, for I felt it would be with but little regret that I should exchange that abode of vice for distant and untried scenes.

After replacing our shoes and stockings, we were placed on board a lighter, where were some sixty men from the Leviathan; and we were soon along side, the "Marquis of Hastings" lying anchored at Spithead, and already containing one hundred men, whom she had brought from Woolwich.

The muster roll was read as we passed over the ship's sides; and on going down to the lower deck, a bundle of bedding was handed to each, containing a wool mattress, two blankets, and a thin rug; all marked with the number, the individual held on the books. Berths were assigned to us, calculated to contain four men, into which we got, waiting further orders. After looking about the hold, the first questions I heard asked by those who came on board with me, were, "what do you get to eat?" and "what is the quality?" exhibiting the all-engrossing ideas of every one's mind. The answer so shocked me, that I was deterred from making any inquiry myself, determined to await patiently, the development of each new scene, without anticipating any. It would be nearly useless to enter minutely into occurrences of that voyage; in fact, it would be too voluminous, and I must be brief.

When the provision did arrive, (which was not until the next day) we found that the breakfast consisted of nothing but the usual "skilly;" the dinner, alternately, of four ounces of very salt beef, and two ounces of plain pudding; or of three ounces of pork and a pint of pea soup; and supper of one pint of sweetened tea or cocoa—one sea biscuit having been issued in the morning to serve for the day's bread. The messes were of six men each, with only a "kid" to bring the food down in, one tin cup, one wooden spoon, and one knife and fork, as table furniture and eating apparatus for the six.

The ship was a large one, perhaps of 600 tuns burthen, and the middle deck was fitted up with two tiers of berths on each side, from *abaft* the midships to the extreme bow, with at least twenty hammocks swung in the intermediate space. The number of prisoners thus congregated in one mass, were two hundred and forty, and the utmost confusion and tumult continually prevailed among them, at all times, except during the silent watches of the night. They were separated into three distinct grand divisions, controlled by as many captains, assisted by a dozen constables, all subject to the surgeon superintendant. These *officers* were all selected from the worst characters the black book contained, all particularly marked by the qualifications so requisite in the government of such institutions, viz: an inordinate desire to obtain a superior's smile—consummate artfulness, with a designing, deceitful, and treacherous heart—a love of human misery, and a disposition to glory in the pain of others. Indeed, it is astonishing how familiarity hardens the heart of man to human suffering, and steels it against all the strange and ghastly things of terrestrial existence; but ten times more astonishing is it, to find men who appear, without such terrible training, to feel a pleasure in the sight of sorrow, and derive a sort of agreeable excitement from witnessing the pangs and miseries of others. Such beings we must ever hate, and involuntarily shrink from their contact, with as much apprehension as from the sting of a scorpion. The consequence of being under the surveilance of such beings, were the horrid castigations with the inhuman *cat*, of some thirty or more during the voyage, in the manner, and with nearly the same effect, as that of poor Cavanaugh's, on board the hulk, and various other minor punishments, as solitary, double irons, deprivation of food, &c. &c.

On arriving on board the transport ship, 12th March, I lost no time in writing to London, requesting the attendance of Mr. Waller, who arrived on Friday, the 15th. seemingly under great excitement of feeling; yet, to calm our minds relative to this sudden transportation, he said he "expected it would be so, to ensure the safety of those whose cases were undergoing investigation." I had long imagined such was the feeling, and therefore made but little complaint myself, only anxious that some of our letters for America, still in their hands, might convey the intelligence to our friends; and that he would exert himself to restore our clothing. He left promising to attend to our requests, and return on the Monday following, as the ship, he was informed by the superintendent, would not sail until Tuesday. Of his promised aid, and the restoration of our clothing, books, &c. we were deprived, by the ship sailing on Sunday, the 17th March.

You, my dear sir, are, doubtless, as much surprised as we were, at so sudden a departure, for so distant a land, contrary to many assurances, made, no doubt, in deceit, for no other purpose than to cajole unfortunate beings into hopes, a depression of which must aggravate their misery an hundred fold. Thus ended all our trust in British clemency; and thus, in eager, anxious destitution, we commenced a voyage of 16,000 miles, to the Antipodes of our homes, in connexion with a mass of corruption and crime to which the world could scarce find a parallel.

Here were beings from almost every class in England—those born to wealth and honor, and those possessing the Queen's commissions not excepted. To the eye of the man of perception, it would have been curious and interesting to trace the aspect of those wretched men, the effects of their imprisonment and transportation, under the various circumstances, upon each character. And although every man plead "not guilty," to any charge of crime, yet it was easy to discover what had been the misdemeanor of either, by their manner, and by their private stories for entertainment, during the fore part of the night. There you could hear the tale of the light debauchee, who had received his doom for some criminal intrigue—of the highway robber's hair-breath escapes—the burglar's artful triumphs over stone walls and iron bound chests—the cunningly devised, and skilfully executed plots of the sly pickpocket—the wily gamester, *sans* principle, *sans* feeling *sans* every thing but a love for crime and iniquity—the bold, daring, brutal criminal, hardened in offences, and impudent in crime —the man of deep feeling, bowed down by a sense of evil and shame—the dull, heavy man of guilt and despair, who could tell of many years imprisonment and exclusion from social intercourse; with the "light of hope gone out of his eyes," and nothing left but tenacity of life and capability of endurance—and of the youth, who, in a passionate excitement, had sought to poison himself and betrothed, fatal with the latter, because parental authority interposed obstacles to the ill assorted union. Thousands are the anecdotes that I could relate concerning that ship's cargo. I will not, however, detain you with them; but proceed with relations of more of the horrors of the passage. On the embarkation the weather was cold, but as we approached the equator, it gradually became more and more warm, until intense heat rendered our situation not only inconvenient, but shockingly uncomfortable. The hospital incumbents were daily increasing, until the salt waves closed over thirty unhappy victims of cruelty and starvation. Vermin, the most loathed of all objects to an American, generated too, in such abundance, that our beds and clothing became literally alive with them. My dreams were always about them, and I would often awake in the act of killing them. They remained with us during the voyage —they landed with, and still separated not from us, until we were *assigned* in the country, where it was extremely difficult to get rid of them. Oh, my dear sir, you cannot conceive the slightest approach to the torment we endured while subject to these ruthless invaders of human comfort— those *implements* of exclusively British torture.

You will say this picture is disgusting; but if the relation is revolting to the mind, what sensations must have been engendered by a participation in the reality. Ah, many nights did I spend, without sleep or rest, while my ever busy mind would roam over the wide world without motive, and assume a tone but little short of distraction—when every noise was hushed save the lashing of the waves against the ship's sides, the creaking of the helm, the occasional tread of the crew on deck, or the heavy breathings of the human beings about me, has my heart experienced every vicissitude of human misery and passion—sorrow and grief, gloom and despondency, anger and the extreme of despair endured to an extent seldom felt by man.

The erysipelas or scurvy broke out among us, and continued to carry off the poor fellows, long after we had landed; so that one year from the date of our arrival out of the two hundred and forty persons, the Marquis of Hastings was freighted with, only *one hundred* and *three* were alive; owing, as declared by the skilful surgeon of the Colonial hospital at Hobarttown, to nothing but ill treatment—short and bad rations.

From Spithead we had a very fair wind, until we entered the Bay of Biscay, when we were driven back to the coast of Ireland; yet we soon regained our course, and sailed gently on in sight of the Azores, the De Verds and the majestic Teneriffe. Again high winds drove us out of the general track to the American coast, when, after two or three days spent in fruitless attempts to continue around Cape Horn, the course was changed, and we bore away from the cape of Good Hope, off which we found high winds, rough seas, and foggy weather; where, in a night squall, we lost our jib-boom, and dropped the foreyard, both of which was soon replaced, and we passed on safely, although many fears were entertained for the old rickety craft. Notwithstanding many high gales, she proved a safe conveyance to us; yet her passage homeward was not so fortunate, for she was lost off the coast of China. We passed very near St. Paul's island a small, barren rock, standing one hundred feet or more out of the sea, with no anchorage about it. In certain seasons, a kind of fish is caught in abundance there, very little inferior to our northern salmon. It lies about fifteen hundred miles from Hobarttown, a distance we run in fifteen days.

Embarked on the wide ocean for a long and tedious voyage, I had full leisure for thought; and though amid the tumult of hundreds of beings, scarce human, I suffered it not to disturb me. I felt not of their species, and gave no ear to their confusion. I stood in the midst of a sink of iniquity, and every shade of crime, from the deepest to the lightest die. Surely if there are places in human abodes deserving the title of Hell, one is a transport ship, crowded with felons, culled from England's most abandoned criminals. Statistics show that the number of committals in one year, was eighteen thousand and eighty-three—one thousand three hundred and ninety-seven of whom received the sentence of death. From this eighteen thousand, select a few hundred of the worst, cast them together without moral restriction, and you have a school of vice that cannot fail to instruct the novice in a more elevated course of *artful* crime. Pickpockets formed no small share of the cargo, and they are truly the most expert and deceptive beings I ever met; they would take from under my very eye, the food I was eating, without my discovering the thief.

I steeled my heart against the contaminating influence of all these vices, by pondering, with intensity, upon the past and the future. I chose that course, although it rendered the mind dark and moody, and in unison with the sad objects presented to it, because it shut out the evil associations of the present; though it produced the bitterest blight in nature, a despondency that became awfully convincing of the instability of human enjoyments, the vanity of human pursuits, and the mutability of earthly hopes. The future exhibited a path of sorrow, suffering and danger; a life of toil and slavery and a bed of thorns; while a review of the past pierced my soul with a thousand agonies. My early hopes; the gay dreams of youth, and the associations of riper years were blasted—gone—circumstances loudly exclaimed, for ever!! I saw my poor family, feeble, and destitute, and lonely, and in grief. I raised in my heart a picture that, though creating anguish, I hugged to my soul, and would not have parted with for all the honors and fortunes of the world. I sought for no oblivious antidote, but closely embraced the malady that produced abstraction, rather than partake of the scenes acting around me. But obloquy, severity, and indignity, religion alone gave me strength to endure with proper equanimity, and blunted many a pang, dark, deep, and bitter.

About four weeks previous to arrival, poor J.J. McNulty became very low, by the decline commenced on the passage from Quebec, and greatly augmented by the harsh treatment, bad diet, and filthiness subjected to since. He lingered on until we cast anchor, when he was sent immediately to the Colonial hospital, where he died four hours after arrival, exhibiting a powerful faith and a perfect assurance of eternal happiness. I also showed symptoms of the erysipelas, a disease prevalent on board, every case of which had, as yet, terminated fatally. The swelling of my head, face, and limbs was discovered by the surgeon, who ordered me to the ship hospital, when, by my request, he took a large quantity of blood, and I returned to my berth; the same night I bled also very freely at the nose. The bleeding was effective in reducing the malady, but an inflammation commenced in my arm that soon spread itself over my right side. By inquiry, it was discovered that the lancet, with which the incision had been made, was the same used, a few hours before, in opening a putrid swelling on the knee of a poor fellow, who died in a few minutes afterwards. The fault was not the surgeon's, but the attendant's, who was culpable for not cleaning the instrument. It was attributed to carelessness, but I imagined it was wilfulness, as he had openly professed an extreme unkindness to all my countrymen. He soon fell a victim to the same disease that his heedless conduct had infused into my veins. The flesh of my right side assumed a livid hue, and gradually grew darker. The pain was excruciating, and appeared to proceed from the distention of the veins, which seemed to be filled with balls, continually rolling toward my extremities. The surgeon was hopeless, and spoke of amputation; but, providentially, we arrived at the critical moment, and I was sent on shore to a hospital, where I remained eight weeks under the hands of a skilful and kind surgeon, who happily reestablished my health. The day before we entered the harbor, Alexander McLeod showed violent evidences of a quick consumption, and was also carried to the hospital. He enjoyed a lucid interval of only five minutes, and died in forty-eight hours after landing. When lucid he recognised me, and spoke of his friends, to whom he wished to be remembered. As his pain returned he called on "Mary," and, with a violent struggle, his spirit burst from its clay tenement, to try the realities of another world.

Many others from the ship were sent immediately on shore, and some twelve, or more died in the first week. The anxiety to hasten the landing, will be explained by the fact, that the surgeon superintendent got five guineas for each prisoner he discharged alive, although they might die the moment after; and for all who expired on ship board, he received nothing at all; consequently those consigned to the sea were a *"dead loss"* to him.

I was, as I have before said, in the same ward where poor McLeod died; and though scarce able to move, I saw every scene that followed, which I would fain pass over unrelated, for fear of wounding the feelings of his dear relatives; but satisfied that they are reasonable and reflective beings, and would regard outrage upon a dead body, as in no wise affecting the peace of the soul, yet as the strongest indications of an enormously hardened depravity, and a total want of sensibility in the perpetrators. He was taken, as he expired, stripped naked, put in the "man box," and carried to the dead house, and there stretched upon a table. Five days afterward a body of prisoners, who had come in the Marquis of Hastings, were sent to the hospital to carry away and bury the dead. They arrived and found the body on the table in the ward cut in many pieces, with its entrails lying beside it. They gathered the pieces together and put them in a coffin of rough boards, and behold it was poor McLeod, whom they all knew, and respected. The scene was revolting, but there was no alternative; they carried him away, and laid him in a "strangers grave", without ceremony, or one mark to distinguish the spot from the thousands of "felon mounds" around him. Alas, poor man! he thus went early to his "narrow bed", without one friendly hand to smooth the thorny pillow of death, or wipe the cold dampness from his pallid brow. Without a kind sympathising eye to watch his movements and anticipate his wants. No cheering voice to calm his mind, and point him to the efficacious blood of a Saviour, save him who lay beside him in an agony of pain on the verge of the grave himself; and whose mind was filled with his own griefs. Yet I wept the fate of the poor, noble, persecuted fellow, whom I had, since adversity had cast us together, regarded as a brother, and when I witnessed the expiring struggle of his brave spirit, and saw its clay tenement deserted, I felt a burning, withering, desolation, and thought my spirit must accompany his from this world of care and sorrow. My uneasiness and pain gave so much trouble to the wardsman, (a convict,) that he administered a quieting opiate which threw me into a profound sleep, and from which I did not awake until late the next day, just as the surgeon was, with his dozen attendents, taking his morning round. He enquired for poor McLeod; and on being informed of his removal to number fourteen, (dead house) he said, "I feared it! I wish to heaven I could have saved him; but he came too late for our skill. I never saw as perfect a model of a man as his; and I am sorry to say that I candidly believe him to have fallen a victim to the barbarity of the surgeon of the ship, who ought to be placed in the same situation that a dozen of his men are already in, since landing. If they continue to send them here as fast as they have done lately, all local patients must be excluded." It was, indeed, thus; for in one week from our arrival, all the beds in the building were occupied, and many were on the floor, notwithstanding its ability to contain some two or three hundred persons. When he approached my bed, he said, "And are you too one of the Marquis of Hastings' men?" I replied that I was, and a countryman of the last dead

"What, an American! Indeed I pity you poor men, who are sent here to suffer the horrors of transportation, and be subject to the contaminating influence of the greatest depravity the world ever knew, for what ought not to be considered a crime against God. What ails you?" I exhibited my arm, and told the cause. "What, a foul lancet? In England the fellow would be indicted for mal-practice. You have, however, come in time; I can save you; but, I dare say, he would have either amputated your arm, or have cast you overboard, if the ship had been out three days longer." He ended with giving orders for certain applications, and placing me on "full diet", with extra wine tea and sugar. So, while I remained in that place, I had enough of the best provisions.

A few days after the whole were landed, Mr. Chandler was sent there also; and in ten days, was returned to the barracks. Van Camp likewise came, having been sent out to assist in drawing a cart load of wood from a hill, some two miles distant; in doing which, he was ruptured, and otherwise injured. He, too, died in three weeks after landing. Thus, then, there are but six remaining of the nine Americans, and two of whom were sometime in jeopardy.

But, then, I must conclude; and you can not expect more than one or two letters more upon the subject of our treatment, when I will continue with a description of this country, which is indeed worthy of a more prolific pen and ability, and a more fertile imagination than I possess; for more magnificent scenery, and grandeur of prospect, if mountains on mountains, reared to the clouds with their concomitant, awful precipices, ravines, and forests can be called so.

> I remain, dear sir,
> Yours, &c. &c.

13

Hospital to Ashgrove

To ——,

My Dear Sir: —

I must now go back to the landing, which I did not myself witness, but gathered all the information I could desire from others. The harbour is a very capacious one, and the ship anchored some half mile from the docks where she was visited by the Governor, the Secretary, the Chief, and other Police magistrate—the principal Superintendent, the District Constable, and a whole posse of clerks, with huge folios under their arms —constables with their rattles in hand, numbering at least half as many as were on board. Before the officers the prisoners were each arraigned, questioned, and examined in the manner I have before related as taking place on the hulk.

It is strange, indeed, when the prisoners knew every mark they might have on their persons would tend directly to identify them in case of absconding, (and but few ever performed the passage without having formed some plan of that kind,) that they would, while on ship board, make it their chief amusement to imprint, indelibly, upon every part of their bodies, letters, words, flowers, and a thousand fanciful figures, every one of which was carefully noted in the "descriptive folios". I fancy it would be a great treat to see published, leaves from this and the "character book". To read the whole of the latter, would require more than an age; for the slightest as well as the grossest characteristics of every male and female prisoner ever sent here, are minutely recorded.

The prisoners were all landed *en masse*, and marched to the "Tench", (prison barracks,) and there ranked in the form of a half moon; then addressed by the Governor Capt. Sir John Franklin, after having been formally delivered by G. Jeffries, R.N., Surgeon of the ship, to the Superintendent of convicts, W. Gunn, Esq. The address was a "puffing" one, and very appropriate. Sir. J. told them that he had full evidences of all their former conduct, and pointed out the course they must pursue to wipe off the stains and disgraces of their characters—that it was their fault, that they were reduced to the present degradation—that they must submit to the laws and regulations adopted for their governance, on pain of exemplary punishment — that these had been rendered more illiberal and severe than formerly, at present, by the extreme depravity of their class—that they would be narrowly watched, and the minutest misdemeanor punished, otherwise they would still remain vicious and corrupt. He warned them of the different degrees of punishments adopted to curb and reclaim the refractory. He descanted upon the benefits of "assignment," with *"glowing eloquence"*, and said, "you must submit to the legal control of the masters, for when put in their custody we hold them accountable for your conduct; and if you pass with good conduct your probationary periods*, you will be entitled to the indulgence of a ticket of leave, with which you may choose your own masters and employment, and receive wages; but still subject to restrictions and surveillance; and close upon its heels comes the emancipation, with its *high privileges of* citizenship, and, at last, the *free pardon* from Her Majesty, *God bless her*. These are favors of great import, and worth aiming at; but they cannot be obtained without good conduct."

This speech was a set one, and occupied some time, being delivered with a hesitancy painful in the last degree to the listener. When it was concluded the men were all dismissed, but the Americans, who had been arranged by themselves. To them he then turned, with high invectives, for "offences against God, and all the ties of social government—for treason, a crime the foremost in all the *British code*". He congratulated them upon their escape from "retributive justice", and said, "some of you, while in England, rendered yourselves quite notorious, for writing disrespectfully of the authorities under whose control you were placed, and even of the government. I will have you understand that you are in a *penal Colony* now, where public sympathy will be no advantage to you, and where all the inhabitants will deem it their duty to keep the strictest watch over you—where, for a slight censure of the government, your punishment will be severe. You come with a character for sobriety, morality, and even piety, seldom found here; but all this will avail you nothing, unless you practise the same. I would, therefore, recommend you to abstain from a connection with the other class of prisoners, whose *forte* is unbounded criminality. I can not tell what will be your situation here, for you are sent without special orders, and we are undetermined yet; however, whatever it may be, I hope you will invariably maintain such conduct as to confirm our present good opinion of your *private* characters."

By the advice given in the latter part of his excellency's speech, my countrymen supposed they were to be separated from the felon gang; and they rejoiced in the hope, for they did not comprehend the possibility of otherwise keeping themselves distinct. But they were miserably undeceived at night fall, when they were indiscriminately mustered with the

* Eight years slavery for a "lifer"—seven for fourteen years—five for seven, and other sentences in proportion.

horde into various wards, in alphabetical order—each containing from forty to sixty persons.

It was some weeks before they concluded to *grant* the Americans the privilege of assignment; and, in the mean time, the Superintendent, a shrewd, penetrating person, told them that he had not the right of putting them at work; he would, therefore, leave it optional with them to labor or not; yet he would advise them, *as a friend*, to go out with the gangs, as the work would be light, and the free air would contribute more to their health than remaining shut in the yard. They thought so too and were rather anxious to see the town, therefore went out, expecting, as it was discretionary, that they could remain in at any time; but here they "reasoned without their host", for when *once enlisted, nothing but sickness could exempt them from labor*. The work was quarrying, breaking, and wheeling stone for McAdamizing the streets of Hobarttown. It was not easy employment, but still they found more bitterness attending a "proper submission" to the tormenting annoyances of the convict overseers, who took pleasure in vexing them, for the purpose, most probably, of getting an opportunity of complaint, on account of the distinctive features of their class. Of these, however, after four or five weeks, Waggoner, Vernon, Mallery, and Cooley were relieved, by an assignment to different settlers in the country, leaving Mr. Chandler, who had returned from the hospital and had been made ward's-man, and myself, who still remained there.

I do not know but that I ought to regard the fatality which sent me to the hospital, as a providential circumstance, inasmuch as I there obtained much information that, no doubt, was a great assistance in averting blows often designed for me, by those beings whom I afterward was forced into contact with. Many of the occupants of the hospital were "old hands", (men who had been long in the Colony,) and they sought to induct me into the mysteries that bound together the various classes of prisoners throughout the Colony, that I might, as they termed it, become a "chum" for "old hands", before my time; I was uncommonly tractable, and made acquaintance with many of the general vicious and criminal courses, without "taking the usual degrees". I learned the method they resorted to, to raise the ready for "lush", (drink) and to evade discovery—how they made up the deficiencies of provision, caused by the penury of their masters, by "weeding" them—while the company took turns in conveying the booty to a general receptacle, and the proceeds were thrown into a public purse—subject only to public wants, or the necessities of a "gala" time, such as Christmas, the day following, (boxing day) and St. Patrick's —"holy days" for prisoners, regulated by law. This "weeding" is a practice adopted by the assigned servants of each farm, who steal from their masters, in small quantities, whatever they can dispose of, and "plant" (hide) it, until a sufficient quantity is collected to make up a "swag" (load) for market, when it is sent by the master's *trusty* man, who is always in the secret, to a "cove" (receiver) who pays some thirty per cent of its value in *"shiners, yellow boys,* or *punt rags"*; and another thirty per cent in rum, or "half-

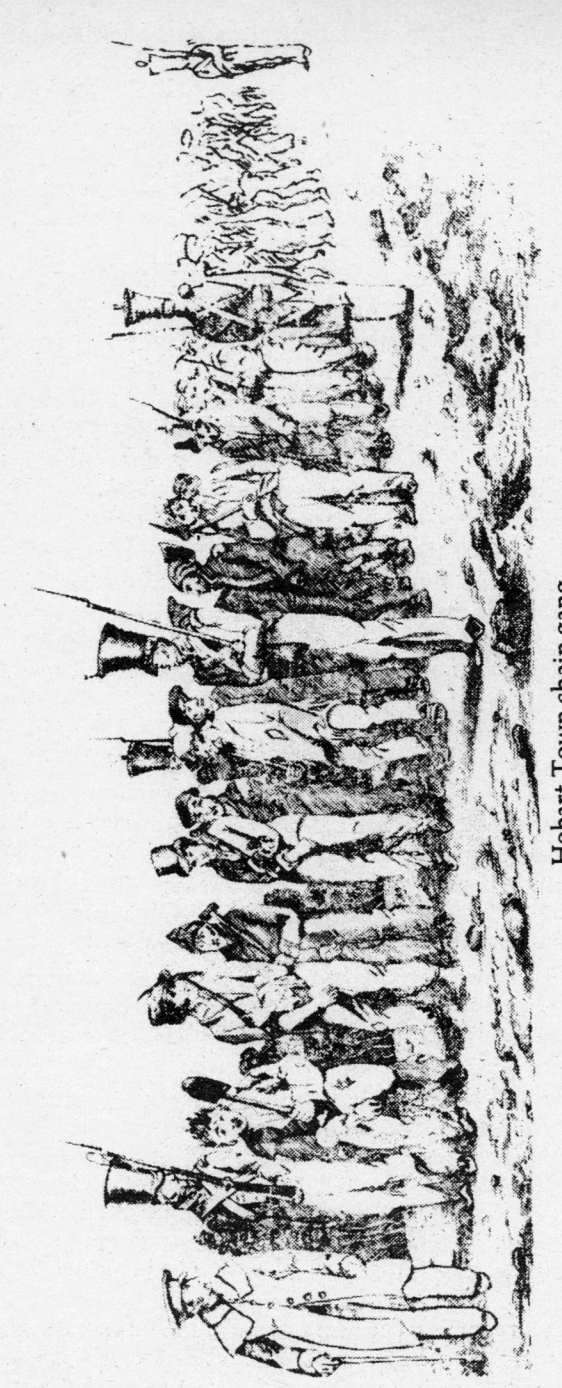

Hobart Town chain gang

and-half" (ale and porter mixed). These removes are always made "under the rose", (in secret) principally when the "bloke" (proprietor) is out. But I hardly saw how such things could be effected, when the country swarmed with constables. "Oh! that was easy enough, as it was a good part of the *trap's* living, for a *crown* would make that all right; and none were *hauled up*, but such as wouldn't *fork over;* and the *cove*, when he discovers any *down* (suspicion) resting upon himself, always makes complaint of having some property *lifted*, and applies for a resident *trap*, who takes the *down* off the place, and all again is *whist*. And, then, when the party has a *down* upon either *pal's* (mate) *coming it*, (informing against them) the *trickster* (a false swearer) makes oath, and the *peacher* gets the triangle, (place where a man is tied for flogging,) solitary, six months on the roads, a chain gang, or, perchance, Port Arthur." These instructions I found of great service to me afterward, for every farm contains such a clique—not that I wished to avail myself of a connexion—but that it enabled me to fathom many of the schemes formed against me, and re-possess myself of such property as had been stolen from what was under my care, and for which I was accountable.

From the Hospital I wrote to England, and gave the letters to an officer of a British ship, who had been confined by the scurvey. I also gave a note, written on the fly leaf of a testament, addressed to Mr. McKenzie, to an American seaman, who was also an inmate for several weeks. From the first of these, and some other letters, I have received replies already.

After two months residence I left the Colonial hospital and proceeded with a pass, to the prisoner's barracks, where my *ticket* obtained me immediate entrance, and I was directed to Mr. Chandler's ward; into which, at twilight, when the outside laborers had come in and supped, were mustered, by Mr. Gunn, sixty men, some of whom were the worst beings man ever beheld. I must pass over this building without description, and only say that it contained some fourteen hundred men, all of whom eat in one room, and then leave you to form your own conception of the manner in which we spent out time in such a bedlam. Constables promenaded the yard and kept the gate, to prevent any thing passing contrary to order. The superintendent's house, and the chapel for the prisoners, fronted the yard, the latter of which had, underneath, a vast number of dark, low, dismal, damp, floorless cells for solitary punishment. A treadmill also belonged to the barracks, upon which some twenty or thirty men were continually "treading" out all the flour of rice, barley, and wheat, that the prisoners consumed and where they slept during their condign sentence. In the yard too, as if to blast the sight of every inmate, stood the inhuman *triangle*, upon which from five to twenty individuals invariably received, each morning, some dozen of lashes *on* the bare back or posteriors.

The provisions were but a trifle better than received at the hulk; and our beds consisted of one mattress and two blankets, almost black with fleas, and alive with lice; while every crevice of the *box* berth, and the wall, was wedged full of bugs. With such companions who could sleep? I could not! so had recourse to narcotics, supplied by the visiting surgeon. I refrain from comment, and permit you to form your worst conceptions of misery, and then say, *you are far short of the real state in which I spent two weeks;* during which time, however, I never was put at work, but kindly permitted to walk out into the town occasionally, and have several interviews with the principal superintendent, Mr. Gunn, a man standing six feet three, and weighing nine and a half score, with a rough, dare-devil look, and a piercing eye; he is wonderfully shrewd, and when having once seen a man, he ever after knows him. He had but one arm, having had the right shot off by bush-rangers, whom, as a Lieutenant, he was, with his company, in pursuit of; this misfortune recommended him to the government, in whose estimation he now stands high, though not at present enjoying the principal superintendency, yet several other offices of emolument and trust.

On the 11th October Mr. Chandler was assigned as a carpenter, to Commissary General Roberts, who also wanted me as a clerk and storekeeper. He had a great difficulty to surmount in obtaining two Americans, as it had been ordered "by the Gov. in council, that none of them should be allowed to remain in a seaport, or two to go to one master." However, by threatening to resign, he gained his point; and therefore, Mr. Chandler and myself were happy in being sent together to his farm, fifty miles from Hobarttown, and seven from Oaklands. The name of the establishment is Ashgrove, and contains six thousand acres of land, on which are some of the most beautiful mountains, sugarloaves, and other scenes, that you can possibly fancy. My duty is to collect, issue, and account for, all provision and clothing wanted by twenty men employed on the place—to keep a minute diary of occurrences—to muster the two thousand sheep, quarterly, with the two hundred cattle, and several horses; at the same time to furnish a most particular description of them—naming every spot—and mark and brand—to keep secure, under lock and key and account for every particle of wool, produce, &c. raised on or coming to the farm—and render a weekly schedule to Mr. R. Then add to this, the duty of a teacher of five children, which had been a part of my vocation for the last six months, and the multiplicity of cares would seem to exclude the possibility of my writing these letters. Indeed I have found it extremely difficult, for almost every moment of my time has its engagement, from four in the morning until eleven at night; but having commenced, it appears now the only amusement I have, saving the monthly letters for my faithful wife, who last addressed me from Canada, whither she has returned, and is continuing her strenuous exertions to effect my complete emancipation. The following is the result of her conduct, of which she had informed me some weeks before I received it.

Principal Superintendent's Office,
3d August, 1841.

MEMORANDUM.

In reply to your application for a Ticket of Leave, I have to acquaint you, that his Excellency, the Lieutenant Governor, has been pleased to approve of your receiving such Indulgence. You will, therefore, report yourself to the Police Magistrate of the District in which you reside, who will take your description, and forward the same to the Muster Master's Office, where the necessary documents will be prepared for you.

J. SPODE,
Principal Sup't.

"ON PUBLIC SERVICE ONLY.
"To Benjamin Wait,
  "Marquis Hastings,"
    "P. Roberts, Esq.,
      "Oatlands."

This indulgence gives me the permission of laboring for wages, and selecting my own employer and labor; but does not emancipate me from the arbitrary "Prison code" or "Summary Punishments." Yet in its enjoyment, I hope to be successful in laying by some funds to assist me to return, in some future day, to my home and friends, if not by permission, on *French leave*. It was procured not only for myself, but also for all the Americans here, who are to enjoy it after two year's servitude, in the capacity of a slave, instead of eight years, which is the usual course. We are indebted to the patriotic conduct and entreaties of my beloved wife, for this slight dawn of liberty. God bless her, and may she succeed in her most ardent wish, according to her heart's desire, is the united prayer of all her countrymen in this ocean bound jail. I will only add, that *my historical* correspondence is pretty nearly closed, and subscribe myself,

My dear sir,
Yours, &c. &c.

14

GENERAL ARTHUR

Mona Vale, near Ross, V.D.L.
Nov. 1841.

To ——,

My dear sir: I will now speak very briefly of the discovery, settlement, and appearance of this Island; then give a few statistical details, and close my correspondence, that is, such of it as may be deemed historical. However you may still expect occasional letters, filled, perhaps, with local matter that may interest and amuse you; yet such must be subject to the freaks of my fancy.

As soon as Van Dieman's Land was pronounced, by the British government, open for emigrants, every sort of inducement was held out in England, to incite a tide thither. The concentration of wealth was desirable; therefore, an acre of land, selected by the settlers at will, was offered for every pound Sterling, in money or property, brought into the country—every article being appraised according to its value here, and a schedule by the owner always taken, as proof of possession. The consequence was, the location to single individuals, of immense tracts of land—for instance, the estate I now date from, consists of 50,000 acres, and has, at this time, a stock of 14,000 sheep—1,500 head of horned cattle, and seven hundred horses; but to return. This of course, had the effect of erecting a state of aristocratic independence, little inferior to England's lordlings; and these men, not paying any thing for labor, could not fail in realizing vast amounts of local property; and, consequently, becoming nominally wealthy; but to be brief, one governor supplanted another, until the reins fell into the tyrannical hands of our *ci-devant* Governor Arthur, who drew them so *taughtly*, that many of the prison population fled to the woods—choosing to seek a precarious existence by plunder and robbery, or an unmolified death, amid rocks and gum trees, rather than submit to his high handed control.

(The consequences of Arthur's despotism, are forcibly detailed in the following note, given me by a gentleman who had acted during many years in Hobarttown, for the American consulate, of Sidney, where I became acquainted with him; and who now resides in Boston. On a visit to the west he called upon me in Buffalo, last autumn; and after hearing some of my manuscript, handed me this note, which I substitute for this part of the original letter.)

Buffalo, November, 1843.

My dear sir:
I desire to assure you, that I fully corroborate all you say, in the manuscript you read me, relative to the government and island of V.D.L., where I resided for twelve years. I was perfectly acquainted with the administration of Col. George Arthur, and himself particularly. During his governorship of thirteen years, in V.D.L., he signed the death warrant for fifteen hundred and eight persons, only eight of whom were saved from the gallows, by being sent to a penal settlement, and doomed to a life of toil, in irons far worse than death. I have seen nine hanging on the same scaffold at the same time, and fourteen in one week. I heard Judge Montague, while on the bench, charging a military jury, and the Attorney General, E. McDowal, while pleading for the crown, say, that 'any number of witnesses like these, (such as were then giving testimony,) could be procured for a bottle of rum, or a half crown each, to bring home to any person in the Colony, any crime that might be laid to his charge.' I also saw two natives executed, after having undergone a mock trial, without the least consciousness of what would be the result of what was going on.

I have the honor to be,
Your's Obediently,
Jesse Morrell.

Mr. B. Wait.

These fifteen hundred executions took place on a scaffold he had erected in sight of his own dwelling; and, oh! what a sumptuous treat it must have been for his hateful soul, as he took his morning airing upon his piazza, to have gloated upon those distorted bodies, as they hung suspended from the "lofty gallows", for the whole day, a spectacle for every eye. The executions invariably took place at an early hour, and the first intimation to the citizens was a sight of the corpses swinging in the winds. I must leave it for you to imagine what the crimes of these victims were, for I cannot tell; neither could many of the citizens, for secrecy was an essential part of his summary government.

These arbitrary proceedings were not the only bloody marks of his ensanguined administration; for the range he permitted the convict shepherds and stock-keepers, resident on the interior runs, to give their brutal, diabolical passions, in their intercourse with the seemingly harmless aborigines, together with the insult offered to them by a formal execution of two of their number, produced a horrid scene of savage barbarity on the part of the native, and of exterminating fury on the part of

Arthur. Various plans were resorted to by the governor, to effect his purposes, against the lives and liberty of these foresters; and so effective were they, that out of the six thousand who were known to roam at large, over the mountains and rocks of V.D.L. in search of the game of the forest, or to dig the native bread* on its plains, only eighty now remain; and they are prisoners, cooped up on a small island, where they are continually dwindling away, so that a few years will entomb the last of the Tasmanian natives, and the race will live no more, save on the page of the historiographer, or in the memories of those in whose breasts their wrongs have excited a kind of sympathy, or a disgust for that power which deals treacherously with the aborigines of every clime it visits.

The system of police established by Col. Arthur, is managed on the principle of "set a rogue to catch a rogue," and has been mainly effective in preventing extended connexions for plunder, and in bringing to the gallows, and into other punishments, thousands of innocent beings. When this Governor was recalled, bonfires, the firing of cannon, guns, and various other demonstrations of joy were kept up for ten successive days and nights, while a respectable delegation was sent to read to him an address, expressive of the most unbounded pleasure, for the final delivery from his long continued mal-administration. . . .

I remain, dear sir,
Yours, &c. &c.

---

*A sort of ball that is found in the earth, without vegetation, to the size of from a quart bowl to that of a man's head, possessing, when steamed, nearly the flavour of boiled rice.

SUPPLEMENT.

GOVERNOR GEO. ARTHUR

Is Ordered
H O M E !

LORD GLENELG closes his Despatch as follows :—" I have felt it my duty, to advise his Majesty, that you should be **IMMEDIATELY RECALLED** ; and I have to convey to you, his Majesty's commands, that, on receipt of this Despatch, you will, with as little delay as possible, repair to this Office.   ("Signed)   GLENELG."

TO-MORROW OUGHT TO BE A DAY OF GENERAL

THANKSGIVING !

For the deliverance from the iron-hand of GOVERNOR ARTHUR. We have now a prospect of breathing. The accursed gang of blood-suckers will be destroyed. Boys will be seen no more upon Police Benches, to insult Respectable Men. Perjury will cease to be countenanced, and a gang of Felons will be no longer permitted to violate the

LAWS OF CIVILIZED SOCIETY.

COLONISTS,

The dismissal of Arthur from the Governorship of unhappy TASMANIA, is a BLESSING, that will be felt by the worthy, and be duly appreciated. The Impounding Law, which was made to benefit the great Members of Council, will be abolished. The Turkey and Persian Act will meet with the same fate ; and the Acts of abomination practised by the hirelings, and secret emissaries of the Government, upon the People, will no longer be countenanced.

▶ REJOICE! ◀
FOR THE DAY OF

Retribution
HAS
ARRIVED.

May 22 1836   WILLIAM GOODWIN, PRINTER, GEORGE STREET.   "CORNWALL CHRONICLE"

15

CONCLUSION

In closing this volume, I fain would name and do honor to the benevolent
Americans who delivered me from the horrors of slavery, but am
compelled to pass slightly over the affair, for fear of ill consequences to my
benefactors, who are again on a whaling voyage, and, most probably, will
visit the same port for refreshments; when, should the authorities be
aware of the fact, they would be liable to a heavy penalty; for, under the
present harbor laws, "the master of any vessel, making a port of V.D.L.,
under whatever pretext, must report every circumstance connected with
her cargo, and muster all her men in presence of a harbor master, who will
visit her.

"Also, he shall make the day of sailing known, so that a District
constable, with his posse, may visit the ship and search her thoroughly,
with a view to prevent the escape of prisoners on ship board; who will
remain until the anchor is tripped, and the sails shook out, when the papers
shall be given to the master, and the vessel to the pilot, who will see her
beyond the heads before dismissing her.

"And further, should any fugitive be found secreted, by the knowledge
of the master, the vessel shall be detained until he shall have paid a penalty
of fifteen hundred pounds sterling; otherwise she shall be forfeited and
sold."

These laws are, indeed, so strict, that but very few ever succeed in such
attempts at escape; yet many try it, not however, by the knowledge of the
master. Notwithstanding the almost impossibility of getting away. Mr.
Chandler and myself, both being employed on one farm, had early formed
the design of flying from our prison, at the first opportunity; but did not
very soon find ourselves properly situated for it. In August, of 1841, as
before related we received the ticket of leave, with which we were enabled
to change our residence without suspicion, and lay by funds against a time
of need; we were, therefore, ready to take advantage of the intelligence
communicated, by newspapers of there being, in the port of Hobart,
several American ships; among whom we hoped, one might be found, who

possessed sympathy sufficient to assist us in quitting the island. With that view, Mr. C. procured a "pass" for ten days absence, and proceeded to town, where he was not disappointed in his trust to the warm hearted American seaman. He made the arrangements, and returned; when certain circumstances enabled us to be absent for two weeks without exciting mistrust.

I therefore went direct to the police office and obtained a "pass" for Hobart, where we spent Christmas in safe seclusion; and soon after, hiring a small whale boat, in which, under the disguise of a party for fishing (no one taking us for prisoners) we put to sea, for the purpose of evading the consequences of the strict "harbor laws," with the spot designated, where we could be found; yet it was not until after we had been tossed about for several days, in danger, destitution, and extreme anxiety, that the *proper ship picked us up "in distress!"* and afforded us comfortable berths in the cabin, where we found genuine American hospitality reigning; and, favored by a kind Providence, we were, after seven months, permitted to hail, with unsurpassed delight, the gladsome shores of free America—ever an asylum for the oppressed. I found a generous welcome, amid the owners of the ship, and the friends of the Captain and first officer. The latter a gentleman of Bristol, R.I., from pure benevolence, accompanied me to the falls of Niagara, and "felt unalloyed pleasure in presenting the long absent and lately emancipated exile, to the open arms of an overjoyed family, after near four years absence."

Over the circumstance of our meeting I will draw the curtain of silence, and leave the fancy of the reader to portray it, and then say, I imagine his picture short of the real—while I tender the most unbounded gratitude to all who aided in my flight, and those who have generously ministered to the aid and comfort of my wife, in her exertions, and my child, in her bereavement, during my absence.

After arriving, I found that a Mr. Gemmel had likewise made his happy exit from V.D.L., a month after our escape, but had arrived a month before us. He ascribes his good fortune to the liberty he obtained with the ticket of leave, which in a handsome card to the public, he attributes to the exertions of Mrs. Wait.

Now, in conclusion, I would say to those who choose to read these letters, that, by having already transcended the bounds I had proposed, by upwards of fifty pages of matter, that will no doubt, be more interesting, I have been restrained from doing proper justice to a description of the country, and am under the necessity of breaking off rather abruptly; yet I would intimate, that, at some future day, I may publish some fugitive sketches, with the minute details of my escape—occurences on my passage home—chasing and taking whale—falling in with icebergs, gales, storms and consequent shipwreck—incidents during a residence of a month in South America, amid fairy scenes that baffle description—calms on the equinoctial line, and thrilling anecdotes of a whaler's incidental life; none of which could have been embodied here, as they are, of themselves more than sufficient for a volume of equal extent.

AFTERWORD

It was dark as the steamer *Red Jacket* eased into the Upper Canadian shore. Twenty-six men, carrying 50 stand of arms, disappeared silently into the woods. It was the night of Monday, June 11, 1838; the place was opposite the head of Navy Island in the Niagara River; the men were Upper Canadian refugees and their American sympathizers, come to liberate the province from its British overlords. Their target was the Short Hills, that perpetually disaffected region in the interior of the Niagara Peninsula. Setting up base in the Long Swamp, the invaders avoided the loyalist patrols searching for them, made contact with potential rebels in the Short Hills, and gradually built up their force. By June 20, they were ready to strike.

As with so many of the military actions of 1837-1838, their attack was inglorious, an insignificant incursion. But this reality obscures a greater reality—the seriousness of their purpose, the tragedy of their failure. They had recruited an army of from 100 to 200 rebels and, on June 20, they marched the twelve miles from their base in the swamp to St. John's, the major village in the Short Hills. There a party of mounted troops, the Lancers, sent to investigate rumours of a Patriot invasion, had stopped for the night at Overholt's tavern. Leaving a sentry outside, the sergeant and nine men of the patrol settled down to sleep. It was two o'clock on the morning of June 21 when shadowy figures surrounded the tavern and its sleeping soldiers, figures wearing an improvised Patriot uniform—white ribbons on one side of their hats, cloth cut-outs of an eagle on the other. A startled young sentry spied the intruders, challenged them, and was fired upon for his trouble. Beating a hasty retreat into the tavern, the sentry awakened his commander, Sergeant Bailey, and roused the soldiers to defence.

Barricaded inside the building, the tiny contingent of Lancers held the rebels at bay. In a half hour of erratic shooting, one defender and two attackers were wounded. Neither side, it appeared, could do the other much damage: stalemate. James Morreau, the Patriot leader, ordered his men to gather straw and to pile it around the inn. They would burn the building and the soldiers with it. Bailey, recognizing the reasonable limits of heroism, surrendered. The Patriots marched their prisoners into the woods, stripped them of their food, arms, equipment and horses, and then released them.

This tiny triumph was the rebels' last. As was typical in the fevered atmosphere of beleaguered Upper Canada, the handful of invaders grew in rumour to a great army. Fifteen hundred Americans, it was reported, had poured over the border into the Short Hills to launch the long-feared, full-scale invasion. The lieutenant governor of Upper Canada, Sir George Arthur, hurried from Toronto to Hamilton, where he called out the militia. The citizen-soldiers marched into the disaffected area, Pelham and Gainsborough townships, ready to resist the Yankee invasion. They found, instead of the major battle they expected, that their job was simply to hunt down Morreau and his band of refugees. The Patriots, aware they could not resist overwhelming force, attempted to slip back across the border to American safety, but the militia controlled the crossing points. By June 22, the day after the fight at Overholt's tavern, sixteen rebels had been captured. Among them, Arthur reported to the commander in chief, Sir John Colborne, was rumoured to be Colonel Morreau. Arthur did not believe the rumour. "This man is a Canadian of the name of Wait a remarkably *(blank in manuscript)* person, bold and intelligent."[1]

Both Morreau and Wait, as it developed, fell into the net. Within a week about 36 rebels had been arrested in a manhunt that went on for a month and eventually rounded up 75 suspects. In the Niagara gaol were all of the leaders. The commander of the invaders had been Colonel James Morreau, or Morrow, a 32 year old tanner from Pennsylvania. His chief compatriots were Jacob Beamer, Samuel Chandler, Alexander McLeod and Benjamin Wait, that "bold and intelligent" man. Beamer, as Wait's narrative pictures him, was a crude and brutal man, a 29 year old innkeeper and carpenter from Oakland township near London, Upper Canada. Chandler was a key figure, a man with local contacts who could encourage the residents of the Short Hills to join their liberators; American-born, Chandler was 48, a waggonmaker, and a resident of Thorold. From East Gwillimbury township, north of Toronto, Alexander McLeod was a 24 year old carpenter who had joined William Lyon Mackenzie in the attack on Toronto in December 1837.[2]

And Benjamin Wait. He was captured during his escape, taken at Navy Island, and imprisoned on June 25. A native of Markham Township near Toronto, Wait was then two months short of 25 years of age. He had lived with his family in Haldimand township, on the Grand River, and operated a sawmill. By the summer of 1837, he was a clerk at Port Colborne. His personal movements from that point are shadowy, his story sufficiently contradictory that one unsympathetic historian has called him "a boisterous and prevaricating Upper Canadian agitator".[3]

The best guess is that he fled Upper Canada that summer of 1837, running to the United States to avoid imprisonment for debt; just another of the many victims of the depression which wracked the province that year. Certainly, well before his departure, Wait had a reputation as an agitator, as an "advanced" Reformer. That tendency was reinforced by family ties. His wife, Maria, who would play such a heroic role in saving his life from execution, was the principal heir of Robert Randall, long-time radical member of the provincial legislature. Randall carried a heavier load of official disapproval than most radicals for he had run afoul of some leading members of the provincial elite in a dispute over ownership of some land. It must have been especially chilling for Benjamin Wait, on trial for his life in August 1838, to see on the bench one of Randall's old enemies in the land dispute, Judge Jonas Jones.

Wait may have re-crossed the border in December 1837 to join the western uprising in the London district. That would account for his rapid rise to a position of importance in the Patriot forces which mustered in the United States to liberate Upper Canada after the failure of the domestic risings. The uncertainty about his activity remains, however. He claimed to be second in command of unsuccessful invasion at Pelee Island in February 1838, but some historians have disputed the claim. He was certainly an organizer of the Short Hills incursion, nevertheless, and he certainly languished in gaol after June 25, his life in the balance.

Those captured in the Short Hills raid were tried in a series of hearings between July 18 and August 18. Their fates were decided more by politics than by the judicial process, which was as well for Benjamin Wait, given the bias against him of the sitting magistrate, Judge Jones. The situation was one of total confusion for a period of months. The legality of Upper Canadian legislation on the punishment of foreigners—and some of the Short Hills raiders were Americans—was uncertain. The provincial Executive Council was dubious whether the political situation called for severity or leniency. And the governor general, Lord Durham, did not help by shifting his position rapidly and erratically. In the immediate aftermath of the incursion, Durham disapproved of Arthur's actions in turning the rebels over to civilian tribunals instead of taking "summary measures", drumhead executions, against them.[4] Later presumably assessing the political climate, "Radical Jack" took a more liberal stance and urged clemency for the convicted invaders.

In the result, the politics of leniency prevailed. Although 18 men were sentenced to death, only one—Colonel Morreau—was executed, hanged at Niagara on July 30. As the Wait memoir discusses so eloquently, the others were saved after the representations of Maria Wait and Miss Chandler, daughter of the condemned Samuel Chandler, and after a public outcry. Of the rebels who had crossed over from the United States, 14 had their death sentences altered to transportation for life to the penal colony in Van Diemen's Land, two were commuted to three year's imprisonment in Kingston Penitentiary, one received a 14 year sentence, five were freed without trial and two were acquitted. Again for political reasons, those who joined the rebellion in Upper Canada were dealt with more leniently. One was transported, one sent to prison for three years, six absconded and escaped punishment, seven freed without trial and six acquitted. Another 26, accused of complicity on shaky evidence, were released.

As the legal tangle continued, the fate of those condemned to transportation hung in the balance. It was a delicate issue, for Lord Durham's action in banishing Lower Canadian rebels to Bermuda, and threatening them with death should they return, was held by Britain to be beyond his authority. The dispute led to Durham's resignation and his return to England in the autumn of 1838. The unhappy Short Hills prisoners were shunted about as their cases were argued. On October 6, 1838, those whose sentences had been commuted to transportation were transferred by ship from Niagara to Toronto. Disembarking at the Toronto wharf, they were greeted by a large and hostile crowd which shouted abuse at the men as they were led through the streets to the city goal. The next day they were on the move again, to Kingston and incarceration in military cells at Fort Henry. On November 9, they were herded aboard the steamer *Cobourg,* to be carried to Prescott, where they were chained on the deck of another ship, the *Dolphin,* for movement to Cornwall. The nervous government, fearful of new invasions to free the prisoners, continued to shift them east. After a stay in the Cornwall gaol, they were sent to Coteau du Lac, to the Cascades, Lachine and, on November 17, to Montreal. The next day the weary rebels were moved by steamer to Quebec, where they languished in the decrepit gaol until November 22, when they were hauled on sleds, handcuffed and chained, to the docks to board the *Captain Ross,* the ship which would take them to Britain where the imperial authorities would decide their disposition.

Benjamin Wait was one of the most active in attempting to convince the British courts and British government to free the prisoners. Writing from the Liverpool gaol, where they were incarcerated, to the British radical Joseph Hume, Wait contended that their removal from Upper Canada had been illegal and unconstitutional, that his trial had been irregular and the introduction of evidence improper.[5] The letters and petitions were to no avail; on January 4, 1839, their chains re-fastened, Wait and 10 companions were put aboard the *Meteor* for transportation to Australia. This peculiar drama still had twists. The *Meteor* was driven back by bad weather, the prisoners were held in delapidated prison ships off Portsmouth until, finally, on March 17 the *Marquis of Hastings* bore them off into exile.

Wait would escape from Van Diemen's Land and make his way back to the United States in 1842. He was reunited with his wife Maria in Niagara Falls, New York, where she had been teaching school. Their new life together was short-lived; Maria died in May, 1843, after giving birth to twins. Benjamin moved to Michigan and re-entered the timber business at Grand Rapids. He remained a well-known public figure for the *Letters from Van Diemen's Land,* which he had written with Maria and published in

1843, was the first of the Patriot narratives to appear. Active in timbering and a founder of the journal which spoke for the business, the *Northwestern Lumberman*. Wait was for many years a prominent citizen of Michigan. He died, aged 82, at Grand Rapids on November 9, 1895.

Why had Benjamin Wait and his compatriots risked their lives and fortunes? Conventional historical wisdom would suggest they did so because they were fools and agitators, because they were misguided and misled. The rebellion in Upper Canada, so this interpretation has run, was an unnecessary event in the political history of the country, a political history which was working itself towards responsible government and eventual democracy. The uprising had a negligible effect upon that political history, beyond the disorder and suffering it caused for those involved. It was, then, the logical culmination of the career of the mad demagogue, William Lyon Mackenzie, who was chiefly responsible for all the trouble. The simultaneous rebellion in Lower Canada was similarly unnecessary and misdirected. It was, in the older interpretation which springs from Lord Durham's views in his famous Report of 1839, a struggle of races. The backward French Canadians, unable to compete economically or politically with the progressive English, lashed out in rebellion. Or it was, in more recent interpretation, a conspiracy by a professional elite in French Canada to secure their own economic and political advancement by stirring the ignorant people into revolt.

Clearly Benjamin Wait and men like him would have rejected such arguments. Their view of the cause was summed up by their reaction to the punishment they received. They felt that their sentences, of whatever severity, were unjust. They were unjust almost by definition, because these men felt that they were fighting for liberty and progress and justice. By what rationale should they be punished for waging such a good fight? The relative leniency with which most were treated, the public support which began to emerge for them, the rapid pardons granted to most rebels by 1843, these suggest that much of the Canadian population and even, guiltily, the government, shared in some measure the rebels' self-evaluation.

The rebellions in the Canadas might well have been seen as struggles for liberty for they were part of the wave of "liberal" rebellion which swept across the western world in this period. From the Decembrist revolt in Russia in 1825, to the revolutions of 1830 in western and central Europe, to the Chartist movement in Britain, to the revolutions of 1848 across Europe, people everywhere were striking against outworn autocracies, striking for liberty. Why should Canada have avoided the contagion of freedom, why should the Canadian rebellions be evaluated so much more harshly?

To compare the Canadian rebellions with their European counterparts puts them in context, but does not explain them. The troubles of 1837-1838 in British North America grew out of local conditions and local problems; the rebellion movements developed with their own logic.

The rebellions in the two Canadas were quite separate but interrelated explosions. On the political level, it was hard for many contemporaries to share the rosy view of colonial development that hindsight has given historians. In Lower Canada, politics had become polarized between a popular assembly, dominated by French speaking members, and the appointive branches of government, which were overwhelmingly English. The legislative council, appointed by the governor, the executive council, also appointed, and the governor himself, could check any attempt by the assembly to liberalize institutions, to make the tax system more fair, or to expand the responsibilities of the elected branch of government. The fact that this political division corresponded to ethnic divisions between English and French made the conflict more bitter, but did not cause it. For similar conflicts arose in Upper Canada, where the assembly as well as the executive was English speaking. There the Reformers had gained control of the assembly between 1828 and 1830 and between 1834 and 1836. On each occasion they found their attempts to reform provincial institutions blocked from above, the business of the province brought to a halt by an intransigent executive which checked and vetoed the legislation brought forth by the Reform assemblies.

It was hard to believe, then, that patience would bring political progress, that Canadians ought to wait quietly to receive the blessings of the British constitution. Indeed, one of the triggers for the rebellions was the political regression which marked the years 1836 and 1837. In Lower Canada, the situation had deteriorated rapidly since the French Canadian radicals had presented a series of demands for fundamental democratic reforms, the 92 Resolutions, in 1834—demands ignored by the English authorities. By 1836 the fight between assembly and executive had reached a deadlock and the assembly followed the only course of action open to it. It went on strike, refusing to pass the money bills which would provide the executive the funds it needed to operate. The response of England, in the spring of 1837, was astonishing in its arbitrary violation of the supposed principles of British government. The governor in Lower Canada was given the authority to seize provincial funds without requiring the normal approval by the legislature. Like the Bourbons, it appeared, the imperial government learned nothing from history for it was taxation without representation which had been the rallying abuse urging Americans into revolution 60 years earlier. A British government which would not honour even the most hallowed principles of its own constitution could hardly be expected to be the agent of political progress. Canadians would have to make that progress themselves.

Upper Canadian Reformers were equally shocked and outraged by the course of politics there. In 1836 a new lieutenant governor had arrived. Francis Bond Head, acting on British orders (for the British were always more willing to make concessions to English colonists than to *Canadiens*), took a group of Reformers into his executive council. The naive Reformers thought a great new day had dawned, that there was to be popular influence over executive decisions. They were soon disillusioned and the Reformers resigned from the council. Head, a vain and undiplomatic blunderer, proceeded to pick fight after fight with the Reform dominated assembly and finally, in 1836, to dissolve it and call an election. He then used the full power of patronage and coercion which rested with a colonial governor to swing the election to the compliant Tories. Under the full weight of executive interference, most leading Reformers were defeated, including the chief radical spokesman, William Lyon Mackenzie. Their complaints about the election, including substantial evidence of serious electoral irregularities perpetrated by the provincial government, were carried to England in September 1836 by Charles Duncombe, radical member of the assembly. But the colonial secretary, Lord Glenelg, would not even see the Canadian delegate. It was a devastating experience for Upper Canadian Reformers. Against all evidence, they had held a naive faith in British justice, they had been convinced that the troubles of Canada stemmed from domestic misrule by colonial aristocrats and that Britain, if made aware of the true situation, would rectify it. In Duncombe's reaction to his failed mission, in his bitter disillusionment, can be read one cause of the rebellions. As he wrote to fellow Reformer Robert Baldwin, he now felt that the people of Canada, "if ever they have good government ... must look among themselves for the means of producing it, for they *(British authorities)* care very little for the people of Canada other than as a source of patronage to the Colonial Office. That must be changed."[6]

This mood of disillusionment, this sense of betrayal, was heightened by the coercion of Lower Canada. Radicals in the upper province had the last vestiges of their faith in Britain shattered; if fundamental rights could be stripped from French Canadians, they could be stripped as well from English Canadians. A powerful feeling of political desperation had seized radicals in both colonies.

Economic distress added to this feeling. Lower Canada had been troubled throughout the 1830's by agricultural depression, the attacks of insects on crops and crop failures. Upper Canada was plunged into depression in 1836 by the stoppage of all public works in the province as the result of cutting off of government funds in the dispute between Bond Head and the assembly. To these domestic problems was added the impact of a general international depression in 1837. Benjamin Wait was far from alone in having to flee Upper Canada to escape from his debts.

Economic causes went deeper than the immediate depression. The rebellions in the Canadas, as with all revolutions, were rooted in the economic relationships of their societies. Colonial economies were by their nature exploitive, that was their purpose. This was most strikingly so in Lower Canada where, in addition to the usual exploitation involved in an imperial economy devoted to the export of raw materials, one group had been systematically excluded from the higher levels of economic activity. French Canadians were not part of the dominant economic elite, the system effectively prevented them from becoming so. Cut off from their contacts in France by the Conquest, unable to develop new contacts, new sources of capital, in England, French Canadian businessmen had inevitably given way to English speaking ones. By the nineteenth century big business was not an arena ambitious *Canadiens* would even consider attempting to enter. That situation helped add bite to political controversies. Young French Canadians of ambition, business closed to them, entered the liberal professions, law, medicine. And politics. Politics became a surrogate for business, a way of climbing in society, the power and patronage of politics replacing the status and economic rewards of business success. To find the higher reaches of politics closed off by the English as well was frustrating and enraging.

To the degree that this is an accurate picture of the French Canadian political elite, their agitation was selfish, their movement towards rebellion *was* a "conspiracy" to improve their own positions, not a liberal attempt to improve the lot of the people. Some of the so-called "popular" leaders had little interest in or regard for the people. Louis-Joseph Papineau, the dominant figure in the opposition movement, was a seigneur, a man who owned a great estate on the Ottawa river and whose primary concern was not to help his peasants progress but, rather, to extract the highest possible income from them. Haughty, filled with aristocratic pretensions, Papineau used the rhetoric of democracy but shared few of its basic assumptions.

Yet the rebellion movement in Lower Canada won widespread support, it won the adherence of perhaps 5000 men who were willing to risk their lives for the cause. Unless we are to assume that so large a number were simply gullible and misled, it is clear that the masses who joined the rebellion had their own reasons, their own frustrations, their own goals. The system blocked them as it blocked the professional elite. The seigneurial lands were full and had been farmed for too many generations. The one accessible area of new land in Lower Canada, the Eastern Townships, had been handed over by the government for exploitation to a group of capitalists, the British American Land Company. Habitants could see the dismal prospects for their sons—life on seigneurial lands which would be divided into even smaller and less viable farms, or emigration to the United States. The agricultural difficulties of the 1830's increased the frustration and increased the readiness to take extreme measures in the search for a solution.

This frustration would have been most pointed for established and ambitious farmers with families, for they would see most clearly the potential problems of the future. This is borne out by the ages of rebels. Among identified leaders of the movement, those in business and the professions tended to be young, 40 percent of them under 30 years of age. They were the young men on the way up, blocked by the English domination of business and the executive government. Among rural leaders, however, the pattern was reversed; 76 percent were over 30. They were the established *habitants*, unable to expand their farms, unable to provide for their sons.[7]

That the rebellion was not simply a race war is shown by the heavy involvement of Lower Canadian Irish. At the level of leadership there were men such as Dr. Edmund Bailey O'Callaghan, one of the major organizers and theoreticians of the movement. And among the shock troops were Irish workers from Montreal, men with a traditional hatred of England, men frustrated by the discrimination and exploitation they faced in their working lives. They, as with the French Canadian masses, had their own reasons for rebellion, reasons quite distinct from those of the middle class elites who led the revolution.

There were similar political frustrations for middle class men in Upper Canada, their ambitions thwarted by the local elite at Toronto, the Family Compact. But the frustrations did not have the added edge of ethnic tensions and the economic system was far more open to them than it was to their French Canadian counterparts. They might be driven to more extreme political positions by the intransigence of the Compact, but they would not be driven to the extreme of rebellion.

The leadership of the Upper Canadian movement came from outside the mainstream of the Reform party, from the radical fringe that had for years been at odds with that respectable mainstream. Mackenzie was no Papineau, he had no landed interest to protect, he had no peasants to exploit. Raised in Scottish poverty, William Lyon Mackenzie rejected the economic system which had exploited him and his kind. In the process he developed a romanticized view of independent agrarians, people who operated outside the system of exploitation. This group, the "honest yeomen", was the group he spoke to, rather than the middle class professionals and businessmen. It was characteristic that, in his draft constitution for the independent "State of Upper Canada", which he published in November 1837, Mackenzie decreed "There shall never be created within this State any incorporated trading companies, or incorporated companies with banking powers. Labor is the only means of creating wealth."[8]

Mackenzie's conception of a rural utopia, with no chartered banks, no large businesses, no factories, with direct democracy and easy civil rights, was naive and unreachable. Upper Canada could not cut itself off from the advance of industrial capitalism, from the influence of finance capitalism. Nor was his conception one that was likely to win ready acceptance from the middle class men-on-the-make who made up the Reform party. It could speak, however, to many frustrated farmers in the province. There was a clear geographical and economic pattern to the rebellion movement, a pattern of agrarian frustration. The chief areas of support for the uprising were: the Midland district in the east, the backcountry behind Kingston; the Home district above Toronto; the Niagara district and its backcounty, the Gore district; and the London district in central-west Upper Canada. All were well-settled agricultural areas, areas beyond the struggling stage of frontier development. All, too, were areas where farmers faced difficulty in expanding and fulfilling their ambitions, and in finding land for their sons. They were debtor regions, in debt to pay for land and for implements, in debt to the merchants who supported the Family Compact, in debt to the banks that Mackenzie promised to abolish. As in Lower Canada, they were angered by the land system. Most good land in Upper Canada had been granted away by 1830, to government officials, Loyalists, the Anglican church and that great speculator, the Canada Land Company, which held a million acres of land in western Upper Canada. Along with their compatriots in the lower province, many Upper Canadian farmers were ready to change the land system by whatever means proved to be necessary.

Mackenzie's ideas were not shared by all those involved in the movement. The Upper Canadian radical cause had its sprinkling of businessmen, lawyers and doctors who sought to better themselves by disrupting the status quo. It also had significant support from the landless, from agricultural labourers and some Toronto workers, notably those in the iron trade and the breweries. These men faced directly the exploitation inherent in the economic structures. The existing land system assured that they would never have their own property, it doomed them, in this age before trade unions, to low wages and bad working conditions. There were other characteristics which marked rebels, as well. They were more likely to be of American or Scottish origin, than to be English. They were more likely to be Presbyterians or Baptists than to be Anglicans.

The rebels in both provinces were far from a homogeneous group, coming from different ethnic, religious and economic backgrounds. But they shared certain characteristics. They were men who found themselves blocked from achieving the promise of the New World by a closed and oppressive economic system. They were men who found the levers of political power jammed by a time-worn constitutional structure. They were men who found that, to gain the liberty, economic and political, that they claimed by right, they had to take up guns.

If their backgrounds differed, so did their ideas about what would emerge from rebellion. The middle class leaders foresaw a liberal, laissez-faire society—much like the United States—in which their ambitions would have free rein. Mackenzie, and some of his rural supporters, expected an agrarian utopia of small farms and educated, honest yeomen. Most, perhaps, had no clear vision of the future. Indeed, most probably had no desire to engage in a full-scale revolution. Many rebels later reflected that their goals were much more limited. In Lower Canada it was fighting between the Tory Doric Club and *patriote* organizations which escalated into the rebellion in November 1837. The chief organizer of the Sons of Liberty, the reform society, was Thomas Storrow Brown. Brown claimed that the Sons of Liberty was not created to foment revolution but "...merely to complete an organization that would enable us to act effectively in election or other riots against the Tory Party who were already combined in clubs."[9] Similarly, after his arrest, the Upper Canadian rebel leader, Samuel Lount, contended that his purposes had been quite limited: "... he did not know of any intention to rise in rebellion for more than 2 weeks previous to the Monday on which the Assemblage took place at Montgomery's.... I had no idea it was to be a rebellion. I was informed and led to believe that what we wanted could be obtained easily—without bloodshed...".[10]

Such declarations could be taken as the rationalizations after the fact of losers, especially in the case of Lount, who was pleading for his life. Yet the claims were repeated often enough by enough rebels to be convincing. And they have the force of logic. Few men are willing to risk everything, few men are willing to contemplate treason. But there were enough men, angry enough, to take up arms in a demonstration of force. They hoped to overawe the government, compel it to make fundamental concessions. If they had had time to think about it, they would have realized that their actions did constitute rebellion, and they might have pulled back. But there was no time to think; events, their own anger and desperation, bore them along, plunged them over the edge into revolution.

It all moved with hectic rapidity. In the summer of 1837, furious radicals in both provinces organized protests. Attacked by Tory mobs, they armed in self-defence. Government inaction, the frequent physical conflicts with Tories, these created an atmosphere of near-explosive tension. Then, in the late fall, the explosions came. Fighting between radicals and Tories in Montreal brought government action, orders for the arrest of radical leaders. The *patriotes* fled the city, mustered their forces, and prepared to resist. It was mid-November, 1837. Major battles between the *patriotes* and British troops in the Richelieu valley followed but, after early victories, the rebel army was soon scattered. News of the Lower Canadian rising triggered the rebellion in Upper Canada. Badly planned and worse led, the attack on Toronto in the first week of December was a disaster, easily repulsed by a hastily-assembled militia. An uprising in the London district, planned to complement the assault on the capital, was a similar fiasco. By the middle of December, the internal risings were crushed, their leaders in flight to the United States.

The fight went on for a year, however. The rebels found a ready hearing in the United States where hatred of Britain had deep roots, and where an adventure in the interests of liberty was attractive to many. American support groups sprang up, most notably the Hunters Lodges, which claimed to have 100,000 members at their height in 1838. Frequent invasions, such as the Short Hills incursion, were undertaken, all marked by poor planning and incompetent leadership. Nor were sufficient men available. Americans enjoyed the excitement of drilling and sabre-rattling at the British but few were willing to risk their lives in actual invasions.

The Patriot cause in the United States was further weakened by conflict within the leadership. From the time they crossed the border, the rebel chieftains were divided over the tactics and the goals of the movement. Among the Upper Canadians, the split was seen most dramatically between Mackenzie and Charles Duncombe. Duncombe, the American-born leader of the rising in the London district, was prepared to integrate the Canadian refugees into the American support groups for he saw the proper goal of the liberation of Canada to be its annexation to the United States. This Mackenzie vigorously and angrily rejected. He was prepared to accept American aid, but insisted that the movement must be Canadian directed, and with independent Canadian purposes. Mackenzie went so far as to charge Duncombe with being a paid agent of the United States government.

Divided, dispirited by defeats, lacking effective military leadership, the Patriot movement could only fail. It never succeeded in tapping the large body of support which clearly existed within the Canadas, which needed encouragement and the hope of success before it would join the cause. By the end of 1838, the rebellion movement was dead.

Was it a comic and foolish episode, irrelevant to the real political progress of the Canadas? That is certainly the usual view. The standard history of Upper Canada, by Gerald Craig, for example, is harsh in its final judgement of the rebellion:

Mackenzie and his associates managed to dupe only a few hundred farm lads and other rather simple people, many of whom paid a bitter price for their adventure, into believing that an armed uprising would cure the province's ills. The vigour with which people from one end of Upper Canada to the other rose to support the government showed that in no sense was Mackenzie the leader of a popular movement. His later admission that resort to force had been a mistake was cold comfort to the men and their families whose lives he had helped to ruin and to the reform cause which he had greatly injured.[11]

Such an interpretation rests on a whole set of dubious assumptions. One is that the rebellion movement had no wide popular support. Given the rapid defeat of the internal rising, thanks to its poor execution, it is an assumption which cannot be tested, for only the foolhardy would have rallied to a losing cause. One could argue with equal plausibility that a body of support existed which could not be mobilized because of the fiasco on Yonge Street in December 1837; certainly government observers of the time feared that such support for rebellion existed and might emerge to the surface under certain circumstances. Even the lieutenant governor, Sir George Arthur, shared such fears. In an interview with a captured Patriot leader, Edward Theller, Arthur revealed his anxieties. As Theller reported the conversation, Arthur told him "... that they were disposed at first to use every means they could, to have me executed and that they would right or wrong have done my business, had they not fears of the Irish who were encouraged by some of those who would not wish the government to know that they had any hand in it."[12] One can do no more than speculate on the potential size of the rebellion, based on a reading of the social and political history of the province.

The interpretation assumes, as well, that the rebels were "simple people," people incapable of making political judgements. However, as we have seen, they in fact tended to be men of substance, established agrarians: the only close study of Upper Canadian rebels, of those in the Duncombe rising in the west, demonstrates that rebels on average held more property than their neighbours, were more prosperous than the norm.[13] Whether or not those involved thought they were engaged in full-scale revolution, they were aware they had undertaken armed resistance to the government. And they knew why they were resisting, they knew they were trying to change an oppressive and unjust society.

The argument suggests that the "reform cause" was damaged by rebellion. In 1838 that appeared to be true, with the radicals gone into exile, the moderates tarred by association. But a public reaction soon became apparent, a reaction against the Family Compact and against its Tory allies. They were blamed for the persecutions of innocents which marked the suppression of the rebellion and, more importantly, for creating the conditions which caused the rebellion in the first place. In this climate the Reform party reemerged with new strength, combining French and English liberals into a political force which would win responsible government in the 1840's.

That was one accomplishment of the rebellions. They broke the political stalemate in the Canadas, the stalemate which had left the opposition parties powerless. For the rebellions compelled Britain to recognize the failures of existing colonial governments. The Durham Report, the union of the two Canadas in 1841, the extension of the power of the elected branch of government and, eventually, responsible government—all flowed directly from the shock provided by the rebellions. The rebellions greatly accelerated the pace of political change and in the process hurried along the development of Canada's modern forms of self-government.

Which is not to suggest that rebellion meant the ideas of Papineau or Mackenzie were triumphant. The real victors of 1837-1838 were the men who were uninvolved, the men who supported neither side. The suppression of the rebellions destroyed the radicals, the political factions of Papineau and Mackenzie. The revulsion which followed destroyed the executive elites, the Chateau Clique and the Family Compact. In the 1840's, new forces filled this created vacuum. New business-minded men came to the forefront, modern men, men devoted to the interests of a new capitalist order. On the Reform side, the stereotypical figure was Francis Hincks, on the Conservative side, John A. Macdonald. Partially in reaction to the emotional politics which had produced the rebellions, partially in service of self-interest, they developed a different style of politics, a different sort of state, a different Canada. In this new order, what was good for business was good for the country. Roads, canals, railroads, factories, these were the preoccupations of the industrial capitalist Canada that Hincks, Macdonald and their kind erected.

There was a nice irony in it all. Mackenzie and the members of the

Compact had fought and destroyed each other. They had done so in the interests of their conceptions of the good society, conceptions which differed greatly yet touched at a key point; both sides envisaged a Canadian that was agrarian, that was devoted to values that were non-capitalist. In destroying each other, they left the field to men whose conception of the society was very different, men whose only goal was rapid industrial capitalist development.

While in exile, William Lyon Mackenzie was horrified by what the United States had become. He wondered whether the American-style democracy that the rebellion attempted to create would not have ended up sharing the evil future he saw looming in the United States. He wrote to a friend in Upper Canada despairingly:

It is very fortunate that we rebels of Toronto failed. It has given some of the constitution makers, that would have been, a taste of the working of free institutions, so called, where they are in practice—and has convinced me that the weak part of the American Constitution lies here. The Fathers of this republic are famous for hav'g estab'd constitutions nearly on this plan suggested by Paine—they provided ag't a nobility—a state church—primogeniture & half blood laws—monarch & so on, but corporations, monopolies, banks of issue, they either left untouched, or, if they did not, the judges have so expounded their acts. And this inlet to knavery is unsettling every'g, & giving a mercinary *(sic)* character to a people formed to be an example to the world.[14]

What Mackenzie could not foresee, in his despair, was that it was the defeat of the rebellions which had unleashed these same forces in Canada. The fall of the radicals and their aristocratic opponents left Canada to the mercies of the "corporations, monopolies, banks of issue", to the men of "mercinary character". That was the ultimate tragedy of the failure of the rebellions of 1837.

Michael S. Cross
Dalhousie University

1 C.R. Sanderson, ed., *The Arthur Papers,* (Toronto, 1943), I, Arthur to Colborne, June 26, 1838, p.209.
2 For biographical details on the rebels, see Colin Read, "The Short Hills Raid of June, 1838, and Its Aftermath", unpublished paper read to the Ontario Historical Society, June 1976.
3 J.P. Martyn, "The Patriot Invasion of Pelee Island", *Ontario History,* LVI, 3, (September, 1964), p.161.
4 Public Archives of Canada, Lord Grey of Howick Papers, vol. 2, Charles Grey to Lord Grey, July 8, 1838, p.62.
5 Public Archives of Canada, Roebuck Papers, vol. 4, file xxii, Wait to Hume, December 22, 1838, p.p.7-12, Wait to Hume, December 26, 1838, p.p.32-35.
6 Toronto Public Library, Baldwin Papers, vol. 42, no. 69, Duncombe to Baldwin, September 15, 1836.

7 The figures come from an article by Fernand Ouellet, "Les insurrections de 1837-38: un phénomène social", *Histoire Sociale*, 2, (November, 1968), p.81.

8 Charles Lindsey, *The Life and Times of Wm. Lyon Mackenzie*, (Toronto, 1862), vol. II, p.354.

9 Public Archives of Canada, T.S. Brown Papers, mss. by T.S. Brown, no date, p.2.

10 Public Archives of Canada, John Rolph Papers, vol. 2, Deposition of Samuel Lount, January 18, 1838, p.105.

11 Gerald M. Craig, *Upper Canada: The Formative Years, 1784-1841*, (Toronto, 1963), p.249.

12 Public Archives of Canada, Edward Theller Papers, Theller to "Garry", June 19, 1838, p.5. Anxious reports from government members and their agents are to be found in the *Arthur Papers*, and in such manuscript collections as the Durham Papers.

13 Colin F. Read, "The Rising in Western Upper Canada, 1837-38", (unpublished Ph.D. thesis, University of Toronto, 1974).

14 Public Archives of Canada, William and Andrew Buell Papers, W.L. Mackenzie to Andrew Buell, October 12, 1839, p.p.24-25.